I0842372

ARMED FORCES AND GOVERNMENT

CM KELSHALL

3

WHEN ARMIES INTERVENE

THE EVOLUTION OF CIVIL MILITARY RELATIONS IN DEVLOPING COUNTRIES

AN EXAMINATION OF THE EXPERIENCE OF TRINIDAD AND TOBAGO

CM KELSHALL

Published in Canada by Centre for 5th Generation Warfare Studies and Canadian Association for Security and Intelligence Studies (CASIS)

Cover Picture: Presslab

Armed Forces and Government

Cataloging –in –Publication Data

Kelshall, C.M. (Candyce) 1968-

Armed Forces and Government

Includes bibliography

1. Caribbean Security

2. Civil military relations

3. Trinidad and Tobago Defence Force

4. Armed Forces and Development

ISBN-13:978-1987731835
ISBN-10:1987731832
Third Edition 2018

Edited by AA White
Special Thanks to Serge Bergler, Natalie Archutowski and Peter Rautenbach for Proofreading and copy editing.

DEDICATION

Over One hundred years of combined family military tri-service.

ADMIRAL.RWR Kelshall MOM ED MN TTCG,

CDR JRP Kelshall GSM TTCG

Lt. GTM Kelshall TTCG Air Wing

SURGEON MAJOR C Farnum, British Army

Capt. A.A. Wallis, British Army

And their wives and mothers

who also serve

Gail, Doreen, Gina, Andrea, Linda, Amy, Denyse

And to Rihab, always.

'Bravo Zulu'

Armed Forces and Government

TABLE OF CONTENTS

ABOUT THE AUTHOR

A former Independent Police Advisor to the British Transport Police and the UK Metropolitan Police. She is the President of the Canadian Association for Security and Intelligence Studies in Vancouver, Canada where she is also an Adjunct Professor at Simon Fraser University, School of Criminology. She is a former Royal Navy Reserve Officer and an SCC Officer. She is a former Diplomat and has run a military and police training company which has trained specialist units for over 15 years.

PREFACE

This book is the second part of a series entitled The Military and Developing Countries: Trinidad and Tobago.

It goes into greater depth on the events of 1970 in Trinidad and Tobago portrayed in the first book of the series "Revolution or Mutiny". "Armed Forces and Government "goes into much greater detail than does the first book which sought to answer one simple question which is vexatious in the study of The Military and Development; that of course is the extent to which a national military force can be considered a pressure group within and upon internal state politics.

The text does not concern itself with the Black Power Revolution in any substantial manner although reference to it is inevitable. In addition this subject is comprehensively covered by "The Black Power Revolution 1970" Ryan and Stewart (1995)

This book utilizes some of the research and conclusions of the first but builds upon the findings to give a broader picture of the events. It examines the input of and effect of the military uprising on the Regiment's sister unit The Trinidad and Tobago Coast Guard. It also goes into greater detail on the after effects of the Revolution on the Military psyche of the Nation's Armed Forces.

The intention of the series is to enable an objective view of the events as they occurred while underpinning the discussion with a flavor of civil military relations theory so as to engender a better understanding of why these events unfolded in quite the manner they did.

During the course of the research, revisited after twenty years it became apparent that a great deal had been swept under the proverbial carpet and in some cases history had quite literally been changed by both accidental and willful omission on the part of those whose sworn accounts have proven over time to be untrue.

 It is not the role of the analyst looking back to cast blame or to attempt to change outcomes but merely to comment on what is borne out by the facts and what is not and to do that without judgment. This book also does not seek to glorify any of the actors in the events herein but to understand why certain actions were taken within the context of civil military political theory.

This book also does not seek to be an academic text although couched in the terminology of the subject and I ask that its shortcomings be forgiven given that the events herein are being revisited forty years after the fact and twenty years after first examined. The original research began life as part of an undergraduate degree at the University of the West Indies in the early nineties.

One of the questions not examined in this book and which will perhaps form the basis of future work is the question of why, Grenada apart, the Trinidad and Tobago Defence Force Regiment was the only military unit that overtly mutinied in the English speaking Caribbean during the immediate post- colonial period. Grenada has a unique set of circumstances which fall outside the

14

remit of this book. Certainly the answer cannot only lie in the fact that unlike Barbados and Jamaica, the establishment of a ground force or regiment did not arise from an existing regiment. Perhaps the answer lies in the argument presented in this text. Is the nature of the existing civil/ military paradigm in a developing country the basis upon which intervention becomes a possibility or not?

FOREWORD

The role and position of the military in newly independent post-colonial states has been a complex and vexing one in many parts of the world, from Asia to Africa, to Latin America.

The part played by the military in many new states in these regions has often said much about the institutions of the state as a whole. In some cases, the military has really been the only organised and credible institution in the state, to which end it has ended up occupying the seat of power.

In other cases, as in the situation in Trinidad and Tobago following independence in 1962 which is presented to us here, there has been no clear vision of what the military is there for, and indeed, why it is needed at all as part of the new nation.

In this monograph by Candyce Kelshall, new light is shone on the whole issue of the relationship of the military to a newly emerging post-colonial state. In particular, the spectrum of involvement from interest group, through pressure group and all the way to a player in central government, is analysed and elucidated.

The example chosen is the story of Trinidad and Tobago, on which little has been written on the question of military and state, but which serves as a particularly fascinating and indicative example of where the military sits in the post-colonial age, and how it might react to unfolding processes of nation-building.

This is a scholarly and detailed analysis which bases its treatment of the story on firm theoretical foundations, beginning with a critique of the Weberian concept of the state as the master of physical force within its territorial boundaries.

Candyce Kelshall moves us skillfully from these essentially European concepts of state and nation, to the situation in a newly independent Caribbean state such as Trinidad and Tobago, where notions of what a military should look like and how it should behave have proved to be particularly difficult questions.

The Trinidadian experience is presented in a refreshing and fascinating way. Candyce Kelshall's knowledge and experience of civic life and society in Trinidad and Tobago shines through clearly in this essay, making the story a rich and fascinating one.

Perhaps more importantly, it also offers a new example of the role of a military in a post-colonial state which adds materially to the understanding of how a military might move from a disinterested lobby group within society, to a deeply antagonised and rebellious movement, and back again.

This is an issue which is as topical and pertinent today in many parts of the world as it was in 1962-70, which underlines the value and importance of this study.

Dr. Julian Richards, Deputy Director, Centre of Intelligence and Security Studies, University of Buckingham (BUCSIS) Buckingham, UK,

INTRODUCTION

In a nutshell, civil-military relations in any state or society is best and most simply described as the system of relations that exists between the political and or civilian body of a state and the military body charged with protecting the state from natural disaster, internal and external aggression.

Civil-military relations can most simply be described as the arrangement or type of relations which exist between the civilian or non military segment of the society and the military segment.

From one point of view civil military relations encompasses and concentrates upon the method used by the political elite to contain the political threat a military force is, to its hold on power.

 It can also be the method any number of interest groups within the society use to control and manipulate the society via the allegiance of and manipulation of a military force.

The study of Civil Military relations may also include the study of the relationship between the perception of the civilian segment of society or the general public towards the military forces of the state.

This case study will briefly outline the theoretical considerations of Janowitz (1964) Huntington (1957) Finer (1988) Lider (1983) and Pye (1962) on the concept of civil-military relations. In addition it will put forward a newly fashioned concept of civil military relations as it pertains to the developments in Trinidad

18

in 1970. The aim is to find a reason for the events within the context of a unique civil military relations paradigm. This will be particular to the Trinidad and Tobago experience and goes some way to explaining why this occurrence happened as it did , when it did and why it happened at all in an otherwise historically stable environment.

 In particular the study will look at the resultant outcome of each of the above theorists' approaches depending upon whether a state is a developed nation or a developing one, and upon whether the political system is communist, liberal, fascist or conservative.

Particular attention is paid to Finer's (1988) position that developing countries lack the administrative expertise and understanding of the military sufficient to effectively control or use the military apparatus of a state[1].

This paper puts forward the central theory that this consideration increases the likelihood of military instability in newly independent nations and the creation of a buildup of 'pressure' which itself becomes a constituent in the relationship between the civil and military apparatus of the state. [2]

---

[1] Finer, S. E. (1988). *The Man on Horseback: The Role of the Military in Politics.* Boulder, Colorado: Westview Press. P4-7

[2]Kelshall, C M, (2011) Mutiny or Revolution pp1-3

I have termed this breakdown a 'gap in understanding' and I believe that the consequent inadvertent and accidental doctrine of separation together with the unstated antagonism, in turn, becomes a defining feature of the nature of the relationship between the civil controlling power and the military apparatus. This paradigm is the one which I believe gave rise to the subsequesnt events in the Trinidad and Tobago Regiment Mutiny of 1970.

This book is an attempt to demonstrate the effect this can have on a newly developing and emergent military culture in a newly Independent country.

It also serves as the basis therefore for examining one of the possible reasons why militaries mutiny in lesser developed countries.

Having identified the models, the study will then move on to examine the model/models applicable to the Trinidad Experience and analyze the system of civil-military relations that existed in Trinidad and Tobago, tracing its origins and explaining why and how certain events, specifically the 1970 mutiny of the Regiment came about as a direct result of the type of political-military/civil-military relations that existed from the outset at the birth of the Defence Force.

It is not a full blown analysis of military intervention in politics of third world countries, rather, it will merely attempt to state that because of the manner by which and the attitude towards, the establishment of the military, the breakdown of relations that occurred between the Ministry of Defence and the Defence arm of the newly independent nation of Trinidad and Tobago, was inevitable and predictable.

Another important aspect which is discussed here is an examination into why the Naval element of the Military apparatus did not publicly and overtly join in, participate or indeed condone the uprising of the Army. In fact the Coast Guard went on to quell the uprising.

A fuller more detailed account of the actual events of the Mutiny within the larger context of the Black Power uprising in Trinidad and Tobago in 1970 can be found in "The Black Power Revolution" Ryan and Stewart.(1990)

Militaries are not by nature prone to take over countries or revolt and it is important to appreciate that when such stirrings begin to develop they do so because of a breakdown in communication either within the military or between the military and the civilian elite governing and controlling it. It is outside the normal realm of action and behavior and is an exceptional circumstance when and if it does occur. This book is about one such exceptional occurrence.

SECTION I: THE MILITARY APPARATUS

CHAPTER ONE: THE MILITARY APPARATUS

The members of the military are best defined as violence management specialists. Within the state the military and military force ostensibly has two roles, an external and an internal one. The external functions of the military are as follows:
-

a) Defence against external aggression
b) A deterrent against any form of war
c) Coercion as a means of backing negotiations of any kind in the name of the state.
d) A protective structure behind which other institutions of foreign policy, economic and politics can operate safely.

The domestic or internal functions of a military force include:-

a) To protect the peaceful and normal course of social life in the stable periods of social development
b) To support the rule of the governing body and to defend it during periods of serious challenges and dangers.[3]

---

[3] Almost immediately this brings to mind the actions of the Egyptian military during the occurrences of the Arab spring in 2011 and the role played by the military in the downfall of the existing political group. It is a perfect example of a military while not engaging in overt revolution but is acting as a pressure

23

In a political democracy the competing political elites actively strive to separate the police from the military and to remove the military from the sphere of police functions except during emergencies. In general, in developed countries the armed forces have managed to achieve a degree of political passivity. This is said to be inherent in their internal organization, from the period of enlistment right up to the very pinnacle of the rank structure. The actual training of the military discourages active discussion and certainly active participation in politics.

The military by necessity for survival tends to consciously subordinate itself to the ends of policy and to policy application.

The military partakes in social life only when a group of people engages in activities that exhaust the resources of the police force and when there is no other alternative to prevent ensuing anarchy.

In the Caribbean the concept of joint operational patrols of military and police is widely used. This leads to an entirely separate discussion on the efficacy of the military to carry out the role referred to above if it has been entrenched in day to day aid to civil authorities in routine patrolling. The distance and impartiality and the shock and surprise element of military presence for the quelling and control of forceful and unusual

---

group within the society. For another example See Kelshall, CM "Revolution and Mutiny: When Militaries act as pressure Groups"(2011)

internal violence is dramatically dissipated when soldiers on patrol are a normal visual occurrence.

Current uses of the military by developed countries suggest the roles of the military as follows:-

- Deterrence
- Defence
- Coercion
- Backdrop for negotiations
- Symbol of national prestige
- Shield for other institutions of the society.
- Political Applications
- Political ceremonial demonstrations (during state visits).
- Demonstrations of force as a threat
- Blockades
- Operations to rescue citizens
- Military operations other than war
- Assistance to other countries with natural disasters and national emergencies
- Supporting diplomatic efforts
- Ideological propaganda
- Demonstrations of military force as a sign of the socio-economic and technological advances of the state.

The military is therefore a major part of the state's resources.

Essentially the military can be considered a specialist violence management team. It is made up of professionals who have a distinct responsibility to the state. The military officer is a professional and the professional is a practicing expert working in a social context and performing services essential to the smooth functioning of the society.

The state is the client of the professional and the professional therefore has a social responsibility, since the use of his/her skill against the state can have serious repercussions. This responsibility and a devotion to his/her skill furnish the professional nature of the military officer.

Financial re-numeration cannot be the primary aim of the professional.[4] The members of any profession will obviously share a sense of unity amongst themselves as a group above and apart from others excluded from this alliance.

____

[4] This perspective is difficult for those outside military service to understand and indeed in a study in 1979 by Burnham and Ghust, UWI p34. They state that "The rewards of the calling of the military officer include wealth status and power" Such a perspective comes from a civil service paradigm where youth is rewarded with rank and responsibility much earlier than those in the civil service. This is one of the essential misunderstandings that lead to the breakdown of the relationship between the military and the public servants responsible for administering it.

This separateness originates during the initial period of training and the required development of the high level of discipline that is the hallmark of professional competence in any field. In particular this is a key requisite required for the leadership of men and women along with a personal sense of integrity and a willingness to be bound by the same rules that bind others to your command.

 The duties of a military officer include:

- The organization, equipping and training of this force
- The planning of its activities
- The direction, operation and control of a human organization whose primary functions are the application of violence and the protection of the state and its citizens.

The military apparatus, requires a high order of individual expertise and hires individuals who regardless of their inherent intellectual ability or qualities of character and leadership could not perform efficiently without considerable training and experience. A military officer's specialized skill is neither a mechanically oriented craft nor an inherent art. It is a complex intellectual skill culminating in comprehensive study and academic training.

The intellectual aspect of the military profession theoretically requires a modern day officer to devote approximately one third of their professional life to formal schooling in the skill of their specialization in addition to leadership and the technical complexities of command.

What motivates a military person is the technical love of their profession and a sense of social obligation and responsibility as mentioned above. This motivation is kept in place by society so long as it offers officers continuing and sufficient pay both during their service and after- in the form of access to services.

The primary responsibility of the military officer is to be an advisor to the state. Their job is to advise on the correct actions to take in particular situations regarding the threat or application of violence and to carry out the final decisions of the political power source. The professional aspects of an officer's responsibilities tend to encompass an exceptionally high proportion of time. As a normal consequence of the nature of the work, a military officer lives and works apart from the rest of society and tends to have, as a result fewer non-professional contacts than members of other professions.

Members of the enlisted ranks are subordinate to the officer corps. The demands, skills and training required for an enlisted rank or rating qualifies them for a vocational competence in a trade or specific specialisation. Enlisted ranks are specialists in their own right. They are specialists in the application of violence but not the management of it. This explains the very sharp line of differentiation that exists between the officers and the ratings in any military. The rank structure does not constitute a hierarchy as does the rank structure of the officer cadre.

 Promotion and demotion is much more fluid here than in the officers' rank structure. Rank in the officer corps reflects the professional achievement in terms of one's experience, seniority, education and ability, to a lesser extent this is also reflected in the ratings rank structure but here ability rather than seniority and experience and education tends to prevail.

Bearing all of these considerations in mind it is obviously an inherent responsibility of the state to take care of the interests of the military personnel who take care of the security interests of the state.

It is also an inherent responsibility of the state to recruit men and women carefully, ensuring that those chosen can reflect and live up to the ideas of a military in a peace time situation. Where this attention is lacking or threatened or reduced the balance between the government and the military takes on a radically new perspective and the specter of military intervention arises.

If the professional military person has dedicated their life towards pursuing the training and education to protect the security concerns of the state, and the state in turn does not take care of the individual and the individuals' family then the imbalance that this constitutes has the potential for disaster.

The military as an entity cannot merely leave the employment of the state, it is bound to serve the state, where the state does not serve its (the military's interest) an impasse is created. This is the nature of an implicit bond between soldier, sailor, airman and state.

This implicit bond represents the oath and agreement that the military and the individuals which comprise it are bound to serve the civilian ruling elite and society in exchange for the

29

permission to maintain professionalism in the art and science of military tradecraft and the management and use of force and violence only in pursuit of state interest as directed by the state.

Any violation or perceived violation of this bond raises the likelihood of military intervention in the 'normal' state of affairs. Where a section of the membership of the military feels that there is a lacking on the Part of the state in ensuring their well being and professional development or maintenance, the strength of the bond between the military and the state begins to be tested. This is where the science of civil/military relations begins. The nature of the civil military paradigm in force determines how fluid or how static the scale of response is.

Issues such as late pay or no pay at all, drastic cut backs in finances; a lack of adequate food to feed the members of the forces, etc. are all, especially when combined, indicators of concern and where these indicators are allowed to mount and are ignored or become an apparent norm a critical situation can develop. Finer (1957) refers to this as the "mood" of the military and characterises it as a determinant of the disposition of the military to intervene. [5]

It is a possible military intervention scenario when the question arises as to why a man or woman should risk death daily either at sea, or in the handling of dangerous weapons, in the interest of the state, when the state apparently has a blatant disregard for

---

[5] Finer, SE, "The Man on Horseback" (1957) page 54

the interests of the military itself and the individuals that people it?

Appropriate civil military relations theory for the particular set of circumstances a state operates in becomes crucial in pinpointing and mitigating trigger events and scenarios effectively.

SECTION 11: CIVIL MILITARY RELATIONS

CHAPTER TWO: MODELS OF CIVIL MILITARY RELATIONS

All militaries operate within civil parameters that largely contribute to the determination of the shape which interaction will take. This shape informs the very operational dynamic which in turn generates the environment a military adapts to working within.

Adherence to the model established at the outset of the establishment of a military force in newly independent, ex colonial countries is critical in ensuring the continued stability of the relationship and consequently the relationship of the military to the society it sits within and serves.

There are several recognizable models that are identified from existing military forces in developed countries and a review of these will generate better understanding of the nature of civil military relations and the role this plays in ensuring continued stability in developing countries.

This is particularly critical as within the context of a developing country the expertise and administrative understanding of the military as an entity may not have had time to develop into a functioning paradigm and there may in fact be no prior model upon which to base or create a functioning civil / military relations doctrine. Below are the predominant models in existence in developing countries.

THE ARISTOCRATIC MODEL

This model is meant to explain the workings of the political military elite power structure as it existed in Europe between 1300-1400.

It illustrates the mutual interest of the military and the political elite since both of those power structures were populated and controlled by members of the same social class.[6]

This was possible due to the fact that the low specialization of the military profession at that time made it possible for the established political elite in this case, also the economic elite to have the luxury of supplying the necessary leadership for the military establishment. This practice was enabled as a result of the established practice of one son going into politics while another son went into the military.

With this model in place and accepted as a norm within the ruling segment of society it was possible for the military to embody the ideology and desires of the dominant group in society. This was by virtue of the fact that inherent links such as birth, family connections and obviously a common ideology was shared between the two power elites of the society: the military and the political section. No conflict could therefore create a breakdown or rift between the two power structures, since they embodied

---

[6] Reid, P" By fire and Sword: The rise and fall of English supremacy at arms 1314-1485 pp6-9

the same principles and were very often comprised of members of the same families.

The security of the traditional system was undermined by the development of mass politics and the development of political parties and the corresponding increase in the professionalism of the Armed Forces[7]

THE DEMOCRATIC MODEL

This model is one that is much more easily recognizable to students of contemporary politics. With the exception of incidents where there has been a forceful takeover of the process of government, it is the dominant and accepted model found in most democratic states. This model is characterised by a clear and sharp differentiation between civilian and military elites.

 The professionalization of the military that occurred with the increasing industrialization of the state and the accompanying

---

[7] A good example is as follows: During the period 1794-1807 The Secretary of the Admiralty A. Marsden, in his <u>A Brief Memoir of the life and writings of the Secretary of the Admiralty 1794-1807</u> pp 97" These officers objected to cheap postage being allowed to sea men since reading and writing was bound to encourage men to think, and they even deplored allowing men to subscribe to patriotic collections, a political act which should have been limited to the propertied classes. Also "They took care of their men partly because they were now aware of the dangers of not doing so " Rodger, N. " The Command of the Ocean A Naval History of Britain 1649-1815" Allen Lane 2004

specialization of social roles is what is essentially responsible for the nature and development of this model. In this model the civilian political elite which itself became a specialized sector of society, had a clearly understood and accepted exercise of control over the military. The military's role is seen as being reserved entirely for national defense alone[8] This control existed via a formal set of rules which specified the functions of the military and the conditions under which they might exercise their role within the context of society.

This role was clearly defined as the management of violence and the maintenance of established norms within society. These rules especially exclude the military body, as a whole, from involvement in domestic politics. The military here is seen as a body of professionals in the employ of the state. Their specialized tasks are easily discerned as being distinct from civilian careers and roles. Within this model being a soldier or naval officer or rating is incompatible with the possibility of holding any other social or political role.

This stance is due in part to the training of the military officer which revolved around the indoctrination of the concept that a military man or woman cannot be political in order to best and objectively serve the state he/she is employed by.

---

[8] Ball, A "The Structure of Government"(1983). P203

This is as a direct result of a championed professional ethic for the military officer. [9]Military leaders in this model obey the government because they accept as fundamental the basic notion that civilian authorities exercise power over them.

This view is most easily described as follows: the military is employed by an employer (the state) to fulfill contractual obligations (the oath that every military person must swear to). The military must therefore accept as unquestioned the national and political goals of the democracy which they serve. The professional ethics of the military officer and the democratic parliamentary institution that exists in the state, ultimately guarantees civilian supremacy.

This model is an objective and an ideal and political policy in democratic states move towards the fulfillment of this ideal. What is basic and fundamental to this model is the premise that the military person is strongly motivated by the professional ethics of his/her service.

In many ways the model is conditional so far as the need for the political power structure to keep its end of the bargain is

------

[9] Howard, Michael, "Soldiers and Governments: Nine studies in Civil Military Relations" (1957) pp19"The Soldier was now a technical adviser whose views had constantly to be given weight...he was now an indispensable expert whom even the most suspicious liberal politician had to trust; while the soldier himself had to accept the fact that the politician , whose ideas and personality he as often as not abominated, controlled resources of men ,material and morale without which the most expert of commanders was helpless"

37

important. As with most things in life the military must be satisfied with the conditions under which it works. This criteria is essential and will be examined in depth in the next section. This type of model is also known as the Liberal Model.

TOTALITARIAN MODEL

This model is immediately recognizable as the model along which the Soviet Union[10] and Nazi Germany and Fascist Italy [11] exercised their system of civil-military relations during particular periods in history.[12] Military ethics are universal and as such, are unchanging. Since this is the case then different methods of control must be realized to harness or manipulate the military of each state, according to the ideology which prevails in the state in question.

With respect to the totalitarian state system of civil military relations, the fascist ideology is one that glorifies war and views it as the highest aim of the individual.

In general and particularly in peacetime the military officer is one whose profession is the maintenance and management of peace.

---

[10] Pipes, Richard (1995), *Russia Under the Bolshevik Regime*, New York: Vintage Books, Random House Inc., pp240-281

[11] Gentile & Mussolini (1932)"La dottrina del fascismo"

[12] Payne, S. Fascism Comparison and Definition (1980) UW Press, pp. 73

The military in a fascist state therefore must be infiltrated at certain points to ensure the necessary indoctrination of the military mind to the fascist ideas of war, glory and empire.[13] "When political control of the military is not secured either by traditional, liberal or penetrative means, the danger of a coup is endemic" [14] Thus when the lines of communication between civilian authorities and the military are broken or the continued requests and/or demands, and/or warnings, of the military are not heeded then intervention inevitably occurs.

____

[13] Cowley and Parker (2001) "The Readers Companion to the Military in History" The Society for military history. Boston, Houghton Mifflin pg316

[14] Ball, "The Structure of Government"(1983) P. 203

39

CHAPTER THREE:
SUBJECTIVE AND OBJECTIVE CONTROL OF THE MILITARY APPARATUS

If we extend the thinking of Huntington in Soldier and The State (1957) we can bring forward the arguments around civilian control of the military and address some of the issues which present themselves to developing countries around the concept of controlling the military apparatus.[15]

A better understanding of the theory helps to appreciate why the military plays the role it does in continued uprisings in Latin America and the Caribbean. There are two types of control exercised by civilian governments. These two types of control are Subjective Control or the maximizing of civilian power to ensure military compliance and objective control which is the maximizing of military professionalism.

SUBJECTIVE CONTROL

The subjective control of the civilian government on the military can be accomplished using three main areas of influence: Government institutions, social class and the constitution. When civilian control of the military is accomplished by government institutions it is accomplished using a process of checks and

---

[15] Huntington, S. (1957)The Soldier and the State: The Theory and Politics of Civil-Military Relations Belknap Press

balances. The government ensures the model is built on the premise that political control of the military rests with a centralized and authoritarian political party. The military gives the political elite its support because the political elite 'bribes' it by placing at its disposal significant state resources. As a sign of the co-operation that the power structure is receiving from the military it makes use of the para-military symbols and uniforms (Examples here are El Duce of Italy and Hitler's own quasi-military uniforms) and dedicates itself to the revitalization of the military greatness of the past.

Control of the military is enforced by the infiltration of party members into the military hierarchy as a means of purging those who are not in compliance with the aims of the party. In addition the party will arm one of its own units as a subtle means of deterrence to the military (a practice carried out by the U.S. with its National Guard and in Germany during the second world war in the form of the S. S. and in Russia with the Cheka). The party also controls the system of officer selection. This model is referred to as the Penetration Model and is one method of subjective control.

Huntington(1957) presents a theory whereby the prevailing ideology of a state can also be used to explain the type of civil-military relations that exist.[16] He identifies four main ideologies –

---

[16] Huntington; The Soldier and The State: The Theory and Politics of Civil-Military Relations; (1957)Cambridge, The Belknap Press of Harvard University;

Fascist, Marxist, Conservative and Liberal. He examines the compatibility of the present day professional military ethic with each of these.

An ideology is presented by him as a set of values and attitudes held by a group of people in a dominant position, about the aims and direction of the state's policy. He advances that at no time any one person has total control of the military resources since this would obviously place the control of power by the governing political elite in potential jeopardy. This type of subjective control was also exercised in the aristocratic model whereby class and social standing linked both the military and political spheres. They shared the same values and had the same demographic makeup and this effectively removed any potential danger.

The other important type of subjective control to be found is that of constitutional control, which is best suited to and easily identified in the democratic model. In this model the actions of the military are subject to a series of laws which shape its powers and parameters. Depending on the constitutional form however, any variety of civil-military relations can be envisaged since the constitution would vary according to the ideology of the state. In so far as the democratic model would advocate that the civilian power group hold the reins of control, in the absolutist constitutional model the military has a monopoly on violence and so has a monopoly of power in an arena where control is exercised by force and coercion.

In a totalitarian regime this increase in power by the military is managed by breaking the officer corps into competing units or by establishing specialist forces which intimidate the regular forces.

Since terror, surveillance and force are the methods by which totalitarian governments rule the state then it follows that the military is controlled by civilians by the very same method. In this way the potential increase in power that the military may gain, in its status as the violence management team in such a state is compensated by special methods which once again tip the balance in favour of the civilian elite.

Subjective control therefore achieves its objectives by civilianizing the military, making them the mirror of the state. The essence of subjective civilian control is the denial of an independent military professional sphere.   This concept will be revisited when the Trinidad experience is analyzed.[17]

OBJECTIVE CONTROL

The opposite of subjective civilian control is objective civilian control which is basically the distribution of political power between the political power structure and the military power

---

[17] This is embodied by the statement that the military officer is first and foremost a public servant as any other public servant. This view permeated the Ministry of Home Affairs during the creation of the defence force. Burnham and Ghust (1979) Diploma in Public Administration thesis. University West Indies.

43

structure that allows for the emergence of professional attitudes among the officer corp.

Essentially, objective civilian control has its foundation in the professionalization of the officer corps. It is directly opposed to the watering down effect of subjective civilian control. With the objective control method, civilian control is effectively accomplished by the elevation of the professional military ethic which advocates service to the state and places the military as a tool of the state.

The most important factor in obtaining this pure method of military control is the need to establish an autonomous and professional (completely) military apparatus.

Military power is minimized by this method because the professionalisation of the military makes their role defence specific and less competent in the managing of affairs of state, itself a role specific or specialized job.

In this way the more professional and the better an officer in their job the less competent their efficiency in the political arena. This might be seen as less an argument against the specific skills of the individual and more about the nature of the authoritarian and precise environment where military proficiency thrives. The indoctrination at the training or cadet level reinforces the negative aspect (and legal implications in the form of the death penalty for treason, which is what a mutiny is contrived to be).

The aversion is indoctrinated early in the career and military officers who go on to become politicians at the end of their career or who become politicized during their careers are actually regarded with a level of mistrust in the pure and idealistic embodiment of a society where objective civilian control is the norm. Officers who are seen to be aligning themselves with the views or actions of individual political parties are also viewed with suspicion.

This type of civilian control is the "lowest possible level of military political power with respect to all civilian groups and preserves military power for the military profession."[18]

Essentially the objective of this type of civil-military relations paradigm is that of a professional military at the ready to obey the orders of whichever political party happens to be in power.

If the prevailing ideology of the state is one that is anti military (where the military is viewed as a competing interest group and by virtue of its control of the states means of violence a potential threat, save for its professionalism, which dictates that it stay out of politics) then it follows that the military can only assume political power by sacrificing its professionalism and attaining the values dominant in the society.

In an anti-military society, civilian control is ensured as is military professionalism maximized, by the military openly

---

[18] Huntington, S. (1957). *The Soldier and The state.* cambridge: Belknap press. P83

45

denouncing political authority and influence and leading an apparently weak and isolated existence divorced from the general life of the society.[19]

In the opposite instance where a society is dominated by an ideology which is favourable to the military's own ideology, such as in the aristocratic and totalitarian models, military power may be increased without being in conflict with a high level of professionalization.

Huntington (1957)also advocates that the price of power is high and depending on the ideology, for a high ranking member of the military to be politically successful it is invariably at the expense of the military ethic that guided him/her to the peak of their professional career.

In order to consolidate their political power base they must surrender professional ethics and adopt the values of the prevailing ideology. Previously important considerations such as pride in professionalism tend, therefore, to be replaced by civilian values of wealth and popularity but the concept of service to the state remains embedded.

There is no shortage of examples of retired Generals and Admirals turning to public service but it is relevant to note that,

---

[19] Huntington, S. (1957). *The Soldier and The state.* cambridge: Belknap press. P 83

political model dependent, this is generally prevalent during times of national crisis or war footing. Examples of this are Gen. Colin Powell US (Iraq War and "War on Terror") Adm. Sir Alan West (Counter terrorism Minister UK) Brig J Theodore Trinidad (UNC war on drug gangs) Admiral Hardy Lewelleyn Jamaica (Chief of Police) This development is particularly to be noted in times of crisis or war. As Howard (1957) points out "No longer was the soldier simply the hero to whom a people turned to lead it into battle he was now a technical adviser whose views had constantly to be given weight in in almost every branch of policy"

In strict military terms and outside of times of war and national crisis this might be viewed negatively since the nature of the profession demands out of the profession and forfeits their high military status. The more involved in politics a serving officer is, the less professional they are viewed and the less impartial they consequently become. Interestingly the drive to be of service in a professional capacity is, it would seem, ingrained and the greater the professional success of an officer, the greater the stimulation and the desire for political involvement on completion of a successful military career.

Politics involves power as does the military so that in many ways attaining rank and power in the military naturally influences the officer to seek further power, when one is at the head of one's service, the natural instinct is to link up to the other power holding institution, the government and political arena, in order to fulfill the desire.

Huntington's Five Civil Military Models

Huntington sees five different patterns of civil-military relations each dependent upon the levels of military power of and professionalism and the type of ideology existing in the state. The first model is one with an anti-military ideology and high military political power while the level of military professionalism is low.

Anti-military ideology/high military political power/low military professionalism

This type of model is found in lesser developed, almost premature countries where the military professionalism has been retarded and is at a low level. It is also to be found in more advanced countries where the presence of an immediate threat increases the power of the military rapidly, thus giving very little time for adjustment. This type of civil – military relation prevails in the Latin American states and historically is easily recognized as the relationship that existed between the two power structures in the United states during the second World war.

Anti-military ideology/low military political power/ low military professionalism

The second model is one where there is still a strong anti-military ideology dominant in the state, coupled with a low military political power and a corresponding low military professionalism.

This type of relation is to be found in totalitarian states of both a fascist and socialist strain. It is most discernable in states where the ideology of the society is so intensely pursued that it is impossible for the military to resist the influence of the value system, no matter how drastically they reduce their political power. The ideas of the governing power are indoctrinated into the military power structure to the extent where their perspective becomes one and the same. Germany and Italy during the World War II are examples of this type.

Anti-military ideology/low military political power and high military professionalism

The third model is one of an anti-military ideology (remembering that an anti-military ideology is one which perceives the military's control of the tools of violence as a threat to its own power) that corresponds with low military political power and high military professionalism at the same time.

Societies which are guided by objective civil-military relations and suffer few national and internal security threats will have this type of civil-military pattern. The United States after the civil war up to World War I is the best example of this model.

Pro Military ideology/high military political power /high military professionalism

The fourth model is determined by a pro-military ideology which corresponds with a high military political power and high military professionalism. This model would appear to be a most complex one since it demands an almost contradiction, that of high political power and high military professionalism at the

49

same time, however this is possible in an environment where the state ideology is one that advocates military ethical values.

The state demands discipline, mobilization and an increasing military power, which having at its head a person who is sympathetic to the values of the military ethic and thus promotes the military's needs and aspirations to an important place in national policy. This is best exemplified in my opinion, by Prussia in the Bismarck era.

Pro military ideology/low military political power/high military professionalism

The fifth and final possible model of civil – military relations according to Huntington is a pro-military ideology coupled with a low military political power and high military professionalism. This system of relations is to be found in societies which in the past have promoted and been successful in military ventures and which are dominated by a conservative (aristocratic) ideology that is sympathetic to the military directorates. Such a combination tend to have similar ideas and social interest. It is also a criterion that the society be relatively safe from threats to its national and internal security. The period of nineties before the "war on terror" (a terminology I have great difficulty and hesitation with)best exemplifies this.

These and the above theories serve to highlight the possible types of civil military relations that exist in the developed world up to today, however when we begin to discuss the patterns of civil military relations in the lesser developed and newly emergent states a whole new theory as it were must be introduced simply because of the radically different origins of militaries and politics in the third world.

I have reviewed the position of Huntington in particular so that we can draw reference to the determination of a new way at looking at civil military relations models for the developing country context.

To this end therefore we will examine the ideas of Pye (1971) and Janowitz (1964) on the origins of militaries in new nations and the corresponding types of civil military relations that are possible.

 In summary when dealing with the developed world there are three basic social models, aristocratic, totalitarian and democratic.

Within each of these models, there are basically two types of civil military relations, subjective and objective and their derivatives and an accompanying five possible combinations of relations of all the above. Having examined the developed world and its relations with its militaries, let us now look at the third world and developing nation states.

SECTION III: CIVIL MILITARY RELATIONS IN DEVELOPING COUNTRIES

CHAPTER FOUR: ORIGINS OF THIRD WORLD MILITARIES

Janowitz (1964) distinguishes between non-colonial militaries, ex-colonial militaries, national liberation militaries and post-liberation militaries.

NON COLONIAL MILITARIES

Non colonial militaries are exactly that – militaries which are derived or which are born out of societies that determined their own growth, development and change from primitive society to modern society.

The armies of these states are therefore naturally spawned and embody values and ideas inherent or indigenous to the particular society in question. Most of the patterns or models of civil-military relations given above are designed to explain non-colonial militaries.

Let us now examine the remaining three types of colonially derived militaries.

EX-COLONIAL MILITARIES

These are militaries which have a cadre of modern trained indigenous young officers who were made available at the time of independence to build up military forces for newly independent states. These militaries had strong affiliations to

53

British values and standards. North African new republics especially experienced this. In the French colonies, where direct rule was the order of the day there was considerably less interest in cultivating an indigenous officer corps and instead large numbers of native and local enlisted men were to be found.

In the Middle East the militaries there were not built from scratch, since they came from a tradition where there always was a military presence. Instead they were re-fashioned but the values and standards of the colonial pioneers were watered down with the 'local' traditional approach to militarism.

 The professional standards of the officer corps tended to be very low and more often than not the officer corps became involved in the political process since they tended to be from the same demographic.

This type of army generally emerged after independence and there was an accompanying low level of internal cohesion, due to the confusion which resulted in the implementation of modern military values over the local traditional approach. Janowitz (1964) includes all of the ex-colonial armies who fought World War II under the command of British Officers in this category of military structure.

POST LIBERATION MILITARIES

These are militaries that were mobilized during World War I and II but did not result in the building up of a professional indigenous corps of officers until just before the granting of independence. A tradition of militarism along British lines was therefore in existence, but very much under the 'Colonial' military leadership. Nigeria is a good example of this type of occurrence, and for our purposes, so too was Trinidad. Another feature of this type of model is that during the transfer of political power from British (in this case) to the local political elite positive steps were taken to develop all the necessary institutions of a new nation state including the requirement for a complete and self -contained armed force.[20]

Generally, the police forces of these states were in existence for a long period of time and were efficient and capable of maintaining adequate levels of political stability in the interim while the newly organized military establishment expanded and localized as quickly and professionally as possible. (In the case of Trinidad an army was created in its entirety in less than four weeks)

In the French colonies the difference lay in the fact that the armed forces remained an important link with the French military institution and the French influence maintained by the continued long term presence of adequate numbers of French military officers. The localization of the officer corps was thus a very slow process due to the retention of the strong military alliance between the ex colony and the colonial power.

---

[20] Pierce-Gould, Lt.Col (1962) "Early Days" in Trinidad and Tobago Regiment Journal Vol1 No 1 Dec 1962 "Sir Alexander Douglas-Home when asked about the criteria for being granted Independence replied it is essential that the country concerned has an efficient army, no matter how small, loyal to the legally elected government and an efficient police force"

NATIONAL LIBERATION MILITARIES

Without going into too much detail it is easy to see that armies born in the struggle for national liberation would have a strong, mass political base because of the people's militia type organization they demonstrated. It follows also that even after independence, because the armies evolved out of the quest for nationhood and in fact provided the necessary leadership that satisfied that quest that they would retain a definite involvement in politics as a type of guardian, especially since the leadership of the military, would have a high political profile, due to their involvement in the gaining of independence. More often than not this interest of the military would expand into active political participation and military take-over. Nothing less can be expected since the very nature of the birth of the military force politicized it at inception. An army born out of a national liberation movement cannot be expected to live a divorced and separated existence from the society it delivered from the hands of a colonial power.

In general it would appear that ex-colonial armies are those which promise the least propensity to military intervention. Where they do intervene and become a ruling power group there is evidence that such action was not pre-meditated and that there was an absence of designed militarism (a desire to intervene in politics and follow an expansionist foreign policy).[21]

Pye (1962) asserts that the armies created by colonial administrations in newly developed countries have the most modern and technological organizations and the command of more resources than any other civilian political elite, simply by virtue of the resources at the disposal of the military. In addition to this the military has a method of comparison that facilitates their determination of the level of development of one state against another. [22]

This is because armies by nature are rivals. The absolute and ultimate test of one army's superiority over another is in the ability of one to outscore another in manpower, technology and leadership. The civilian governing structure of a state, on the other hand, has only itself as a comparison, since it does not, by nature of its job and function have to compare with other states' bureaucracies. The soldier therefore has a greater awareness of international standards and developments and is understandably more sensitive to the apparent weakness of his own society. Apart from this, because armies are separate and apart from civilian society they are also better able to 'see' the

---

[21] Kelshall, CM. 2011 Revolution or Mutiny: The Military as a Pressure Group. Antitype Press, London.

[22] Pye, Lucien (1962) in "The Role of the Military in Underdeveloped Countries", edited by John J. Johnson, Princeton, Pr inc e ton Univ. Press

society than those who are within it. The fact that soldiers in developing countries also go abroad for professional training also facilitates their exposure to the state of the development of their fellow student officers and the ex-colonial power's own development as a bench mark against the progress of their military and their society as well.

Bearing this in mind let us now examine the types of civil military relations possible in the third world. According to Pye (1964) there are three types of inter-relations possible when the military intervenes in the political process.

 In the first one the military stands out and above from the rest of society because in a transitional society where the social norms have been disrupted by modernization the military invariably represents the only organized element in the society capable of competing for political power and forming public policy. This situation arises when the military is among one of the few organizations that survives the fall of the traditional culture system, after a period of upheaval. The military therefore is the only really effective political entity in the society.

The second type of situation possible according to Pye (1962) is where the military while formally espousing the need for the development of a democratic tradition woos the public to become its mass support and their monopolizes the political arena forcing any emerging political elite to turn its interest solely to the social and economic concerns of the state.

The third type possible is in fact the most common where the organizations and structures that are essential to the country's democratic process of government exist but are not able to function properly because the process of modernization has been halted midway. The army in this instance in the most organized and modern group in the society and it assumes the function of government and in fact is viewed as a saviour by the public.

On the other end of the scale Janowitz presents the possibilities that limit the military's role to that of the 'mark of sovereignty' while also giving two examples of intervention in politics. With the first three types the officer corps is not at all involved in 'partisan' domestic politics but functions as an institution which symbolizes the independence and legitimate sovereignty of the new nation – which is of course as it should be.

CHAPTER FIVE: MODELS OF CIVIL – MILITARY RELATIONSHIPS IN DEVELOPING COUNTRIES

AUTHORITARIAN – PERSONAL, CONTROL, REGIMES

In this model regimes based on the personal and traditional power of a single person, or the newly developed personal autocracies found in nations at the very beginning of the process of modernization are in control of the political power of a new state. The military is merely a mark of sovereignty and is understandably excluded from domestic politics, monopolized as it is by a single figure. The military here is probably given considerable resources and encouraged to professionalize.

AUTHORITARIAN- MASS PARTY REGIMES

Here the military is also excluded from domestic politics by the power of the civilian authoritarian political power structure. The authoritarian power may be rooted in a one party state under a strong personal leadership. In some instances there is no parliamentary institution. The civil – political and para military institutions operate as a counter weight to the military's small and not fully expanded organizational structure. (Immediately, Mugabe era Tanzania comes to mind). In some instances again the military may have a limited role to play in the organization of the mass party structure.

DEMOCRATIC – COMPETITIVE STRUCTURES

In this model the military is limited to certain functions because of the strength of the competitive democratic institutions and because of the pattern of prevailing civil – military relations which bases the control of the military on the civilian institutions. Civilian control is a concept that is understood by the military. In this model civilian supremacy operates to limit the role of the military particularly because colonial traditions and training implanted a strong sense of self restraint on the military and its leadership. There exists in the states where this pattern of civil military relations is practiced strongly competitive civilian institutions and power groups as well as a mass political party which dominates domestic politics but permits a legitimate measure of political competition. Without question this pattern of relations is immediately recognizable as that which existed in Trinidad and Tobago at the independence period and the period in which we are focusing this study on.

CIVILIAN – MILITARY COALITIONS

When the military expands its political activity and becomes a political block the civilian leadership remains in power only because of the military's passive countenance on active assistance. The extent of the political competition, that was previously at a healthy level decreases and the regime aptly described as a civil-military coalition with both power structures sharing the reins of power. – This model calls to mind Pye's model where the military sees to the external and defence policy and the civilian political elite exercises its prerogative within the economic and social spheres of the society. Because of the intimate role played by the armed forces, the military serves as an active political bloc – in its support or dislike of other emerging civilian parties and power groups.

The military in this situation and because of its monopoly of the state 'means of violence' remains a constraint while the various civilian power groups conceivably receive or pass the batton of power. Invariably whichever civilian group has power does so because of the support of the military. The military in this case can be wood by various interest groups and in some instances act as an umpire between competing political parties and power groups. Egypt after the Arab spring is a good case in point.

MILITARY OLIGARCHY

The military at this point may be forced to establish a caretaker government where conflict becomes inevitable. In this case it may or may not wish to return the reins of power to civilian groups. Understandably civil-military coalitions are unstable and lead to a level of involvement where, as explained, the military is forced to set itself up as a political ruling group.

When this point is reached then civilian competition is repressed and the military, for so long a political umpire, has managed to acquire over a period of time the political know how to establish a successful stable military government.

Janowitz (1964) also envisages a period of time after the military take over where the military leadership sets out to acquire a mass political base and to develop a more organized, broad political apparatus either through the personal charismatic leadership of one general or through an alliance with a civilian group. Fiji under Sitiveni Rabuka comes to mind here.

SECTION IV: MILITARY INTERVENTION AND MUTINY

CHAPTER SIX: WHY MILITARIES MUTINY

The military in many ways is an interest group and a pressure group. It is an interest group because as a whole it has the same desires and aims as the ruling political elite. In general "when a collection of individuals come together to exert pressure or to influence other collections of people for specific objections then this group becomes what is known as a pressure group."[23]

Interest groups act in order to pursue a common objective and the cause of their concerted action is very often to seek "cognitive cognizance so that their world would make sense or adds up to some meaningful and manageable whole."[24] Therefore when an interest group rises to take action it is because the concept of righteousness is missing and the need to alienate feelings of disorientation and frustration and anxiety become omnipresent. Karl Deutsche lists six model values which he says are at the heart of the action of any pressure group:-

- Security
- Freedom
- Integrity
- Dignity

---

[23] Kelshall, CM, (2011) Revolution or Mutiny 2010 page 1

[24] Deutsch ,K.W.(1988) "Analysis of International Relations " page 55

- Legitimacy
- Cognitive cognisance

What is important to acknowledge is that pressure groups form and activate due to a lack of one or more of the above values which has been promised or was previously experienced. Pressure groups are not a part of the government and do not themselves seek to govern the country in their own name, but do seek to influence the government for their own purpose or cause. Deutsche (1988) sees the military as in fact being "another general purpose group in many countries either as a single group or somewhat divided into several services."[25] As a pressure group, the military in its interaction with civilian society and the political elite has four types of approaches to take in order to attempt to satisfy the missing components of its day to day existence. These four approaches are:-

1. Constitutional approaches of briefings, meetings discussions and commissions of enquiries.

2. Semi-constitutional approaches of influencing civil servants to a particular way of thinking through gifts, luncheons and entertainment.

3. The Semi-direct approach which includes refusals to cooperate in administrative tasks, and holding back on

---

[25] Deutsch,K.W.(1988) "Analysis of International Relations " page 56

information that is normally given freely, also in extreme cases the actual non-compliance with requests and orders, by conveniently forgetting or misfiling or misplacing orders and reports.

4. Direct action. This is the ultimate measure or final resort and includes the withdrawal of labour and the strong possibility of violence.

GTM Kelshall sees lobbying as the main method of the military achieving its goals in the political arena and at the same time sees the mutiny as an extreme method of political pressure that becomes necessary only when the lines of communication become blocked or are non- existent to being with.[26]

Communication breakdowns occur and when there is a problem with the ministerial body above the military and the military hierarchy. This problem can escalate to the level of intervention when all other methods dealing with it or rectifying it proves useless. In fact Robert Dowse (1969) sees military intervention in any form "as aspects of the same phenomena. They signify failures, small and large of the political system". [27]

In simple words intervention implies a breakdown in communications between the governing body and the military

---

[26] Kelshall, G.T.M. "Ten Days in April", Unpublished

[27] Dowse, R. In Leys, Colin, (1969) *Politics and change in developing countries: studies in the theory and practice of development;* London: Cambridge U.P., Pp221

interest group and as explained at the end of Section I of this paper where there is a breakdown in civil-military relations, there implies a lack of attention or concern on the part of the ministerial body which, represents the state in ensuring the needs of the military are met.

The arrow is pointed to the ministerial body because the very fact that the military is a professional body, in the employ of the state means that problems will occur when the terms of the contract are not, or appear not to have been met. The military ethic of professionalism demands nothing less than perfection in the carrying out of the assigned task and this can only be accomplished when they are provided with the right or sufficient tools to accomplish their assigned task. When this does not occur the military interprets this as a threat to their professional reputation and their professionalism since they cannot, as a result, adequately carry out their task. This role of the military is only ever interrupted by flaws or breakdowns in the political system.

It is easily understood then that economic problems and turmoil conditions tend to increase the likelihood of the military intervening in politics especially when it has reached a level of frustration with the existing circumstances that can no longer be contained or dealt with through traditional methods. Dowse (1969) once again comes to the forefront in his belief that frustration within the military produces aggression in the form of intervention or mutiny which can itself be classified into different levels of intensity in terms of the military's reaction to the conditions and frustrations within and around it.

CHAPTER SEVEN: THE TYPES OF INTERVENTION

Direct military intervention in a political process is an exception rather than a norm in liberal democratic states due to the evolution of a system of checks and balances which were discussed in the preceding theory section of this paper where we saw how military intervention was mitigated against by a code of control and an understanding between the ruling civilian elite and the military apparatus. Where there is a breakdown in this relationship military intervention in the social and political life of the country becomes likely. It is important to appreciate that when such stirrings begin to develop they do so because of a breakdown in communication either within the military or between the military and the civilian elite governing and controlling it.

Militaries also usually will have an internal hewing where a split will occur between sides and one side acts against the government while the other remains a "loyal" force. Finer (1988) presents the concept that there are six modes of intervention. He lists them as :

1. Normal constitutional channels

2. Collusion and or competition with civilian authorities

3. The intimidation of civilian authorities

4. Threats of non-cooperation with or violence towards civilian authorities

5. Failure to defend civilian authorities against violence

6. Violence against civilian authorities[28]

These stages however do not adequately explain how the military and its individual constituent parts reached a point at which intervention or pressure was required or arrived at as an antidote to perceived ills.

This paper puts forward the suggestion that there is a stage missing from Finer's classification which is the stage before the military begins to act cohesively and in silent agreement that the bond between civil authority and military has been broken. This suggests that the actual first stage occurs within the military apparatus itself. This stage is Internal Intervention.

THE INTERNAL PATH TO INTERVENTION ACTIVITY

This classification is a concept which is outside of traditional thinking on military intervention mode which tend to focus on intervention activity either after a schism within the ranks or as a unified cohesive whole which acts in concert breaking the bond between civil controllers and military apparatus. Theorists tend to consider the actions of the military as a unified whole in the characterization of intervention. This approach does not adequately explain how the military apparatus came to that place

---

[28] Finer, SE, (1988) *The Man on Horseback*, Praeger, Colorado pp 127

in time or came to the point Finer (1988 refers to this as that point at which motive, mood and opportunity presented itself.[29]

The Internal Intervention action however is not one which occurs suddenly. It is also scaled in intensity ranging from overt internal grumbling and indiscipline on one end to direct mutinous activities of insubordination involving firearms and internal individual violence. It comprises a series of actions which individually seem like random acts of indiscipline and consequently a recruitment or training problem. However when these acts occur in concert with external pressure on the relationship between civilian authority and military hierarchy and during a period of social upheaval or general disorder external to the military they should be characterized as internal intervention activity. These actions are not aimed at the overthrow of the existing governing body as the actors of Finer's (1988) classification eventually aim for. These actions are also by no means the first in a series of steps towards the establishment of a military government, rather they reflect a degradation in the standard of discipline due to a breakdown in the belief system and strict adherence to the internal hierarchical structure which governs military related activity. These structures provide the parameters and a series of checks and balances within which the regulations set out the code of conduct for an environment where firearms and violence are in use daily. Where these codes of conduct and adherence to the system begin

---

[29] Finer, SE, (1988) *The Man on Horseback*, Praeger, Colorado pp20-76

to be eroded one act of insubordination at a time and unnoticed or disregarded it is usually a good indicator that the required standards are not being adequately monitored and consequently the professionalism which Huntington[30] (1962) affirms[31] is the one protection of civilian authority is slowly being undermined. This activity is termite like in action and progression. Where traces of it are ignored or considered acceptable the damage escalates as minor transgressions begin to become acceptable and then viewed as normal until a single catastrophic action suddenly reveals the extent by which the code of conduct has been eroded.

In short, mutinies do not happen overnight. There are usually significant indicators for professional members of the unit to acknowledge and recognize over a period of time.

Once this has internal intervention has begun to change the fabric of professionalism within the military apparatus, only then will the classification of Finer's (1988) modes of intervention become realistic and relevent. The unit as a whole operates in collusion in the knowledge that intervention activity will bring them into direct conflict with the civil authority or the internal intervention catastrophic end game is played with an all-out mutiny immediately prior to national intervention action.

---

[30] Huntington, S.P (1957) *The Soldier and the State*, Harvard pp74

[31] But with which Finer (1988) disagrees in Finer, SE, (1988) *The Man on Horseback*, Praeger, Colorado pp21

EXTERNAL INTERVENTION

There are three levels of intensity that define the type of intervention undertaken. These are loosely aligned to Finer (1988) modes of intervention referred to above. I have changed them somewhat to simplify them. They are limited intervention, direct intervention and military take over.

LIMITED INTERVENTION

In a liberal society the military can advise the government on courses of action that it deems necessary to maintain its interest in the service of the state and it may also lobby the parliamentarians and ministers.

 It may also prepare papers and discussions on issues affecting it as a whole. Assuming that this interest which the military has flagged up is finally taken notice of and action authorized to rectify it, then no additionally intense level of pressure is required. If this is not the case then the next level of intensity in order for the military's cause to be taken notice of is that of direct interference.

DIRECT INTERFERENCE

This is not in fact the assumption of power by the military but falls just short of this. It is basically the military "exerting direct pressure to attempt to achieve a particular political goal."[32] This

---

[32] Ball, A. (1983) Modern politics and Government page 27

73

type of pressure can take the form of a voiced threat or the mere indication that a voiced threat is forthcoming as evidenced by the unavailability of certain facilities that are normally at the government's disposal. There may also be an increase in exercises and military preparatory drills in open areas where the availability and prowess of their specialist skills in violence management can be exhibited deliberately and seen by all and thus act as a silent warning of an extreme kind.

On the extreme end of the scale of direct interference lies small internal grumblings, unusual and unanticipated acts of indiscipline and cases of willful disobedience amongst the other ranks and sporadic incidences of junior officers' insubordination, including non-compliance to given orders.

These indicators all precipitate the possibility of serious problems developing within the internal structure and with the communication links that exist between the army and the civilian authority immediately above it. These signals of escalating indiscipline must be addressed immediately before tension within the military builds and the rest of the unit catches the disease.

TOTAL MILITARY TAKE OVER

This is the next stage after the extreme direct intervention of the military it is exactly what it states and is the situation where the military attempts to assume the control of the government and all its functions. Military takeovers generally occur only when there is a total breakdown in the social order, and periods of uncertainty and mass confusion.

CHAPTER EIGHT:
MOTIVES FOR INTERVENTION

Finer (1957) distinguishes five classes of motives which lead otherwise well-functioning 'servants of the state' militaries to go through the above mentioned steps. They are nationalist, class, institutional, ethnic and personalist.[33] I have broken these down to Internal and External factors. External factors are drawn from the work of Putman(1967) Internal factors that spur the individual to intervention were overlooked in the original analysis of Intervention motives by both Finer (1957) Putman(1967) and Huntington. At best recent studies have focused on what motivates rebel recruitment as it pertains to civilian actors (Weinstein 2007, Humphreys and Weinstein, 2008).

INTERNAL FACTORS

Internal factors are those factors which originate in the officer or enlisted man for reasons which affect his or her own experience of military and social life as a member of the military apparatus of a state.

---

[33] Finer, S. E. (1988). *The Man on Horseback: The Role of the Military in Politics.* Boulder, Colorado: Westview Press.

NATIONALIST

This type of intervention occurs based on an individual officer's perception or conception of the national situation. Invariably he/she sees something going drastically wrong and takes it upon his/her self to rectify the situation. Such an officer if not relatively high ranked and thus having the corresponding resources at or under his/her command, tends to be a natural and charismatic leader and a good orator and is thus able to influence those men and women immediately around or under his/her responsibility. An excellent example of this motive for intervention would be Sitiveni Rabouka's 1987 military takeover of the Fijian islands. In this case Rabuka cited both nationalist and ethnic reasons for the overthrow.

CLASS

This type of motive occurs when soldiers act on behalf of or in alliance with special social interest. Class motivated intervention would occur when members of a particular class within the rank structure of the military perceive the interests of their class to be threatened within the society due to civil disturbances or particular legislation which is disagreeable to them. An attempted total military takeover would most likely occur, influenced by this motive, if the model within which the intervention occurs is aristocratic or conservative. In the example of The Japanese Satsuma rebellion in 1877 this action is taken by members of the Army who resigned en masse and joined together in violent rebellion against the Government to protest changes to the structure of society as it pertained to Samurais.[34] The episode marks the end of the samurai era and pinpoints the beginning of the 'new' Japanese Imperial army based entirely on conscripts.

ETHNIC

The motivation for intervention based on this type tends to originate in religious and or regional alliances. Ethnic tensions that exist in the society, especially multi-racial societies feed the motivation especially in periods of civil unrest or disturbances which may or may not be ethnically motivated. In any instance where members of the military feel that members of the society of their race or religion are being discriminated against in a serious manner then this type of intervention will be motivated. According to the methods of recruitment different militaries will have a greater propensity towards this type of intervention. The military mutinies in Nigeria in 1966 and India 1984[35] in addition to Fiji in 1987are examples of this.

---

[34]Ravina, Mark (2004). *The Last Samurai: The Life and Battles of Saigō Takamori.* Wiley.

[35] Barua, Pradeep. "Ethnic Conflict in the Military of Developing Nations: A Comparative Analysis of India and Nigeria." *Armed Forces and Society* 19.1 (1992): 123-137.

PERSONAL AMBITION

The fourth motive for intervention more often than not results in a total takeover of the machinery of government. This is not necessarily so with the other motives for intervention because the implementation of a military regime is not always required to achieve the aims of the military pressure group (which the military becomes when it is motivated to seek its own interests, in the absence of attention from the ministerial structure above it) in the same way that violence and mass demonstrations are not always necessary to achieve the objections of a civilian pressure group.

Personal ambition motivated intervention, is intervention by the military in the political process, led by one charismatic leader who, for one reason or another wishes to consolidate his or her military power by ensuring that no institution can take it away. The most obvious method of achieving this is by a total military take over. The takeover of Ghana by Fl Lt Jerry Rawlins is an example of this as is that of Gen Idi Amin in Uganda.

INSTITUTIONAL INTEREST

This motive is one of the most powerful for inciting intervention thoughts and active dissatisfaction on one end of the scale and actual intervention actions on the other end of the scale.

Threats toward the institutional interest of the military include (and these may be real or imaginary):

- perceived interference with the professional autonomy of the military apparatus

- perceived threats to the existing living standards of its members as a group

- perceived threats to satisfactory working conditions and equipment safety

- perceived threats to the upwards promotional channels as a result of Government or political interference or patronage or promotions over the established seniority line which are perceived as unwarranted or a liability to the professional interests of the organization as a whole

- perceived interference by civilians in determining the standards of leadership they believe appropriate

- and finally and most importantly to the soldier or sailor, interfering with the timely delivery of his or her pay.

This motive is also known as corporate interest and is the single motive which can most easily unite the military to action against the state which it perceives is the author of its dissatisfaction. This dissatisfaction can be expressed initially in several ways in particular, as disobedience to the stated orders of superior officers who represent the sanctioned power of the state.

When one has signed over one's life training for and being in service to one's country, one expects that this will be appreciated and rewarded by the state. When this concern for, or interest in the needs of the individuals who form the military community appears not to be forth coming then the threat of intervention becomes very real. Apart from these motives Putman (1967) also contributes four external factors that can further influence intervention[36]:

- Certain aspects of socio economic development
- Certain aspects of political development
- Certain characteristics of the military establishment itself
- Foreign influence and contagion

Each of these however has already been touched upon briefly. Having grounded ourselves with the basic theories of civil-military relations and understood the role of military force in society and why militaries mutiny we can consider ourselves equipped to now go on and examine the Trinidad experience with civil-military relations.

---

[36] Putman,R.(1967) "Towards Expanding Military Intervention in Latin American Politics" in *World Politics 20:83-110* .

SECTION V: THE TRINIDAD EXPERIENCE

CHAPTER NINE: THE MILITARY TRADITION IN TRINIDAD

Trinidad's military traditions are predominantly volunteer in nature in so far as the volunteers have a consistent history which dates back to 1797. With the exception of formal fulltime detachments which fought in both World War I and II, the local military tradition has been carried by the various volunteer units established since 1797, when the first military force was founded in Trinidad.

Shortly after Sir Ralph Abercromby became Governor of Trinidad, the 1st West India Regiment was established and recorded in the London Gazette of 02 May 1797. (Ellis, 1885) [37]

Shortly after this the Trinidad Militia was formed in 1802. The foreign Colonial Regular Garrison troops were repeatedly struck down by and depleted by yellow fever, hence the reason for establishing a Trinidad Militia in the hopes that local men would better be able to withstand the conditions on the island. One of the very first units of this Militia was the St. Joseph Light Infantry Battalion.

The principal role of these militias was to help defend the island from the consistent attacks by the French and Spanish regular

---

[37] Ellis, Major, A.B. The History of the First West India Regiment , 1885

forces, and to preserve the coastal towns from repeated privateer attacks.

During 1831-1834 there were over twenty-five (25) units of troops. These included, among others, the St Ann's Hussars, The Royal Trinidad Artillery, the St. Joseph Light Cavalry, Savannah Rangers, The Royal Trinidad Light Infantry, Mayaro District Battalion, The Cedros District Company, Royal Trinidad Battalion, Arima Pioneer Corps, Diego Martin Chasseurs and the Couva and Carenage Battalions.

Training for the battalions and companies was once a month for drill and musketry practice. Parade grounds in port Spain were Brunswick (now Woodford) Square, Fort George and the end of St. Vincent Street.

The barracks of the West India Regiment, on Nelson Street was destroyed by fire in 1808 and the Fort George Barracks was destroyed in 1846.

Fort Picton was located on Laventille Hill and was also known as St. Davids' Tower (having been named after the patron Saint of the Welsh Governor Sir Thomas Picton). This symbol is actually the origin of the six pointed star adopted by many of the volunteer units and used by the present day Regiment.

The corner stone of the St. James Barracks was laid in 1823 and the uniforms were differentiated according to whether the units were infantry or artillery. The infantry wore scarlet uniforms with green facings and the artillery, blue uniforms with scarlet facings.

83

In 1854 the regular foreign garrison troops were withdrawn from Tobago and by an act of government a corps of volunteers was begun in the same year to ensure the defence of the island. In 1879 a Royal Commission of Defence was appointed and construction of a drill hall on Tragarete Road begun.

In 1898 the Trinidad Rifle Volunteers of Artillery was established and consisted of nine companies of infantry with four in Port of Spain and one each in San Fernando, Arima, Princess Town, Couva and Tunapuna. By 1902 the strength was six troops of Cavalry, a Battery of Artillery and six companies of infantry, headquartered in Port of Spain at the St. James Barracks.

At the beginning of 1914 the name was changed from the Trinidad Rifle Volunteers to the Trinidad Light Infantry Volunteers and in addition to Mounted and infantry units there was a bicycle company and a Motor Cycle platoon. (Volunteers had to supply their own bicycle and motor bikes). One of the members of the Trinidad Light Infantry Volunteer Motor Cycle Platoon was a Trinidadian who became the highest ranking officer of the Royal Air Force, Air Vice Marshall Claude Vincent, C.B., C.B.E., D.F.C., A.F.C., Silver Star of Serbia.

At the outbreak of war in 1914 the volunteers were mobilized and those who did not join the merchant contingent or the West India Regiment instead carried out Defence duties for the duration of the war as a type of National Guard.

The Merchant Contingents of 1914 – 1917 were so called because merchant firms in Trinidad put together to defray the cost of transporting troops overseas. During World War I seventeen

(17) contingents of volunteers were sent to England to fight for Britain and twenty-two (22) Military Crosses were won by the members of those contingents.

After 1918 most of the units were disbanded except for one company of Light Infantry in Port of Spain and a troop of Light Horse in San Fernando. In 1920 yet another battalion was formed as a reserve unit.

In 1937 during the civil disturbances the Trinidad Light infantry Volunteers and the Light Horse Troop were called out to quell the disturbances and to maintain the law and order. In 1937 the Light Horse was disbanded and a machine gun company implemented in its stead, it still carried the same Light Horse unofficially however.

In 1938 the 2nd Battalion Trinidad Light Infantry volunteers changed its name to 1st Battalion Trinidad Volunteers of which Brigadier Joffre Serrette COV, MEB, ADC, was a member. Joffre Serrette went on to become the Commanding Officer of the Trinidad and Tobago Regiment. He offered his services to the Prime Minister during the ten days in April when the army insurrection was ongoing. On completion of the disturbances he became Chief of Staff of the Defence Force and established the first Head Quarters of the combined Services.

At the outbreak of World War II the 1st Battalion Trinidad Volunteers was mobilized into full time service while the 2nd Battalion maintained its part time status. Once again as in World War I the volunteers served with distinction in the British Armed Forces overseas.

85

The 2nd Battalion Trinidad Volunteers was disbanded after the war in December 1943 and the 1st Battalion followed suit in 1948 and its colours laid up in Trinity Cathedral.38 After this point the most significant military happening was the formation of the West India Regiment which began recruiting in September 1961 to form the Federal Defence Force. Recruiting for the force was carried out on a percentage basis according to the population of each of the ten islands of the federation.

By 20th September (the death knell of the Federation) two hundred Trinidadian and Tobagonian nationals were serving in the West India Regiment.

When the Federation ended serving members of the West India Regiment were given a choice of options: -

Nationals of Jamaica and Trinidad could either join the Jamaica Defence Force or the Trinidad Defence Force or opt for a discharge.

Nationals of the Leeward/Windward Islands could either join the Trinidad or Jamaica Defence Forces or the British Army or take a discharge.

One hundred and fifty of the Trinidadian nationals serving in the West India Regiment opted to join Trinidad and Tobago Regiment in addition to fifty nationals of the other territories. Approximately two hundred soldiers who were already trained

---

38 Phillips, D. *Another Look at the TTDF* 1994 p3

therefore were made available to the newly formed Trinidad and Tobago Regiment.

The first regular unit of soldiers in Trinidad was in fact left under the command of Thomas Picton who had a garrison of one thousand and forty-seven men within which were Colonel De Soter's Black Corps, the first regular Trinidad military unit.

The unit numbered only forty men and came to be known eventually as the Royal Trinidad Rangers who formed the nucleus of the 10th West Indies Regiment. In response to a series of threats by French and Spanish Privateers Picton commissioned his own Coast Guard, whose only unit, a launch by the name of The 'Barbara' was 60 feet long, had two masts and eight guns.

The crew was predominantly black ex-slaves loyal to Britain. The whole crew in fact was totally local and they were the fore runners to the Sea Fencibles, a volunteer naval unit begun in 1803. Trinidad and Tobago's naval tradition thus originates with these brave men, the first Coast Guardsmen.

CHAPTER TEN: ROLE OF THE MILITARY IN TRINIDAD

In the third world militaries cannot be expected to merely exist, waiting as it were in the event some natural disaster or war should occur to justify its presence especially where that military was a colonial legacy left over from the retreating colonial power.

In instances where the military of a third world country has not participated in the liberation movement of the nation it is especially important for it to be given a role whereby it can cultivate public attachment and generate feeling from the nation.

In Trinidad the regiment was fashioned after the British Army in what was seen at the time to be the finest traditions of the departing Colonial power. The young regiment strove to match their high levels of efficiency, discipline and morale.

As far as the general population was concerned however this military force and its very concept was as alien and remote as the Colonial power's London Capital. [39]

---

[39] "They (the military) were a hazy group you heard about now and then and saw on parade at Independence time" The Mariner 1987 pp126, Jacqueline Winter Roach

It's existence was a requirement to the granting of Independence. This was one of the major problems in the formation of the military apparatus at Independence. Its distance from the very people from whom it was recruited and among whom it should work and whose interest it should serve.[40] It was almost as if the views of Samuel Adams were wholeheartedly embraced by the new Government. Adams believed that a standing army, "however necessary it may be, is always dangerous to the liberties of the people,"[41] In keeping with that view the Military was located on the very end of the island on the peninsula of Chaguaramas.

In a third world emerging state the luxury of an idle army awaiting its moment to act simply cannot be afforded. It is not politically intelligent as events proved, nor is it economically feasible to have the centre of a nation's human and technological resources lying in wait for a big event, while the rest of the society endeavours to complete the task of nation building.

According Major Selwyn Derick, (ret'd) of the Trinidad Tobago Regiment "It is sacrilege not to tap a resource so well prepared

---

[40]Spencer , J. Capt.   MOM.BAB (UWI) Problems Pitfalls Possibilities.   An analytical study of the Military in Trinidad and Tobago. Chaguaramas 1974

[41] H.A. Cushing, (ed) *The writings of Samuel Adams* [New York: Putnam, 1907] p250

89

and available."[42] In his view a newly formed regiment, should immediately have been put to work in nation building for two major reasons:-

To build public attachment through visibility

To effectively remove the danger of boredom and frustration when the novelty of military life begins to wear off.

A syndicate of Defence Force officers in 1974 identifies these same points and emphasized that it was crucial that "in a developing country the Defence Force should make a viable contribution." They felt that the military role should "in a large way be one that contributed to the development, economic stability, social upliftment and manual labour problems of the nation as a real contributor and should not be dependent."[43]

In developed countries, especially the one the Trinidad and Tobago Defence Force was patterned after, the military was a force geared to fight aggressors and in peace time, due to their laurels, were accepted by the public as dependents. In Trinidad the military was an institution that was forced upon the

---

[42] Derrick, S. Maj. 'The role of the military in developing countries 'Unpublished Trinidad 1987

[43] Syndicate 11 The TTDF from inception to 1974. Pp 5

Independence seekers to begin with. It was a condition of Independence.[44]

The fact that it would be a dependent, based on the role given it and not contribute to national development in any tangible way was just another black mark against it that further alienated the political elite, and as a consequence the mass public. "The Trinidad and Tobago Regiment, given these circumstances seemed almost destined for problems."[45] It was a mysterious hidden institution suddenly scrambled together. For not other perceptible reason, than that it would guarantee independence. "The Trinidad and Tobago government cannot have wanted it. They showed far too little interest in its formative stages to have really cared about its development." [46]

In fact as evidence of the unimportance placed on this guarantee of sovereignty the Prime Minister visited his new Defence Force only once in the eight years between its inception and 1970, and this occasion was as a result of a request from the Queen of England on a state visit.

In most new developing nations the army is considered to be the primary source of pride, power and prestige as was the case with Nigeria where the military literally came to personify

---

[44] Shah, R in Ryan, S., The Black Power Revolution a retrospective, ISER 1995

[45] Kelshall GTM Ten Days in April Unpublished pp26

[46] ibid

91

Independence and prior to 1966 was the well loved and respected child of the nation. In Trinidad and Tobago quite the opposite was the case and this was due essentially to a total lack of understanding and of meaningful communication between the ministry and the military.

 The Defence Force, short of three functions :-

Defence against external threats

Aid to civil power

Internal security of the territory

Was given no policy directive in terms of a day to day functioning role, in fact once established and present for the Independence Day parade and the country granted its much coveted Independence, the Army and the Coast Guard, seen as nothing more than a means to an end, were left to grow, experiment and survive as best they could. The politicians followed closely by the rest of the nation who took their lead, viewed the military as an unwanted child. The politicians did not understand it nor did they appear to know what to do with it."[47] This situation had a very obvious in that the people responsible for establishing the best type of civil military relations for the new ministry of Home Affairs and the young Defence Force, was the average civil. He in turn answered to the politician above him and invariably neither of them had ever served with a military or national service unit.

____

[47] Spencer, J. Maj. The military in Trinidad and Tobago p.7

And so the task of creating and maintaining a new Defence Force was assigned without any prior consideration or care as to the special needs or aims or objectives of a military in a developing nation. Given this type of auspicious start in the perception of the civil servants responsible for nurturing the civil-military relations of this young state, it would appear as though future problems were candid for the future from the very birth of the army. The most important aspect in the birth of any military is a healthy civil-military relationship. In the case of Trinidad this was not even a consideration. The military's existence was merely a means to an end. In addition to this the lack of foresight into the value of a military in a developing nation further worsened the situation in that the invisibility of the armed forces from the general public, who were paying taxes to support it, only aggravated an already bad situation. The military here did not give any vital leadership to the acquisition of Independence, hence the need for them to have been given a more comprehensive highly visible role in developing the country which would have allowed them the chance to earn public affection and respect especially since, they were viewed as a colonial legacy from a colonial power, whose shackles the nation had just managed to free herself from. In this vein the Officers Study Day Syndicate of 1974 questioned whether "the British approach to militarism was the correct one for Trinidadian culture and whether or not a more flamboyant meet-the-people approach would have worked better."[48]

____

[48] Syndicate II, Trinidad and Tobago Defence Force Officers Study Day "The Defence Force From Inception To 1974"

CHAPTER ELEVEN: ESTABLISHMENT OF THE TTDF AND MISTAKES MADE AT ITS INCEPTION.

In 1961 Trinidad and Tobago announced its intention to press for Independence. This remark was met with a response by the crown that forestalled any such action until Trinidad and Tobago acquired "preliminary defence action in order to fulfill one of the pre-requisites of Independence in the means of defending oneself." [49]

In March 1962 Earl Mountbatten of Burma Chief of the United Kingdom Defence Staff held talks with the Premier Dr. Eric Williams where it was established that United Kingdom military personnel would be made available to Trinidad to plan the Defence Force and to provide initial leadership "until such time as local personnel had been trained and would take over." [50]

On the 21st of March 1962 the Ministry of Home Affairs formed a small military planning committee. The role of the Defence Force was set out as :-

---

[49] Eastwood,B J Lt. Col."Early days" TT Regiment journal vol. 1 no. 1p. 5 Dec 1964

[50] Eastwood,B J Lt. Col."Early days" TT Regiment journal vol. 1 no. 1p. 5 Dec 1964

Internal Security of the territory

Assistance to the civil power in national emergencies and national disasters.

Defence against external aggression.

These roles had been recommended by the British planning team and reflected their knowledge of how a military force's role was perceived in developed countries.

In addition to the role, the military planning committee recommended the formation of a British type infantry battalion and a small sea going force of four coastal launches. Both were to be military units and both were conceived as being part of one Maritime unit since Trinidad was an island state with a lot more water around than land on it. This last recommendation the government dispensed with.

The target date for the acquisition of both these units was August 31st 1962. This was required so that the two units would participate in and be ready by the grand Independence Day celebrations. This gave a grand total of just under four months from concept to formation of the Defence Force. Both the rapid creation, newness of concept and cost attracted criticism as the unit establishment was allocated 8.4 million dollars vs the 1.2

million dollars allocated to other state departments such as Community Affairs."[51]

The first battalion of the Trinidad and Tobago regiment was duly formed on July 23rd 1962 and comprised 211 members of the defunct West India Regiment and 21 senior officers and other ranks form the British Army. Lt. Colonel Pearce Could was designated the Officer Comanding the 1st Battalion Trinidad and Tobago Regiment (TTR) and Commander Peyton Jones the Officer Commanding the Coast Guard's Office in London to form the land unit and the Coast Guard's genesis was the Marine Division of the Police Force. "Having agreed the establishment of the force, the question of recruitment to fill it was examined and in view of the short time available before Independence (months) it was thought that short cuts must be taken to fill some of the vacancies in order to make a viable unit."[52] Ex service personnel and others with some military knowledge were to be recruited and it was necessary to draw up short service schemes both for officers and other ranks as in all cases the men were too old to join on normal terms."[53]

---

[51] Burnhum and Ghust., A Study of the Role of Trinidad andTobago Defence Force 1982 UWI p4

[52] Eastwood,B J Lt. Col."Early days" TT Regiment journal vol. 1 no. 1p. 5 Dec 1964

[53] IBID

97

The uniform committee was organized to determine what the unit's uniforms should look like and to do this the committee examined past practice in Trinidad to determine which colours, cap badges and crests should be adopted. In this manner Trinidad's own military tradition was taken into account rather than simply copy what existed in the West India Regiment.

The infantry battalion would incorporate one regular unit and a volunteer unit with the regular providing the shock troops in the event of internal security trouble, and the volunteers a reserve. Three rifle companies of reserves and three of regulars were envisaged. The United States provided $600,000 US to facilitate construction of both temporary and permanent accommodation. The site chosen was a purely political move on the part of Dr. Williams in his tireless attempts to remove the American presence in Trinidad. The United States Base of Chaguaramas was thus appointed as the site of the headquarters of the land units. The Coast Guard remained in the existing Marine Police division at Staubles Bay. It was also determined at that time that the Commander of the Defence Force would be the Commanding Officer of the Regiment. This decision by the ministry of Home Affairs, in one fell swoop determined the superiority of one force over another, in what was initially designed to be a Defence Force of two units of equal structure. It effectively informed future professional officers of the Navy that they could only travel so far in their career and that they would be inferior to all army officers who could aspire to the rank of Commander Defence Force, which they the navy could not.

The two units immediately set to work building a Defence Force and in the words of a soldier who correctly understood the whole motive behind the establishment of a Defence Force, "our Task was to prepare for Independence and that meant drill"[54] In the absence of any other day to day role, this, essence this was exactly what the regiment did until its mutiny in 1970. August 16th saw the commissioning of Major Hylton Edwards, Captains Christopher and Mc Conie and Lieutenants Grannum, Goddard and Halfide in addition to a Cadet Officer Second Lieutenant Brown.

The acknowledged short cuts that would have to be taken in the recruitment process was perhaps the biggest mistake of all. No immediate attention was paid to the quality of men recruited, but attention paid to the quantity that could be attracted in time for Independence so that a sizable force could be presented to impress the crowds and to provide to the Crown of England that jumping the obstacle of providing a means of defence, required little effort at all. One of the subsequent mutineers of 1970 Lt. Raffique Shah made a statement on the recruiting process in retrospect, his views are perhaps an understatement as to the types of people the regiment recruited in its hurry to be ready for Independence "every cook, driver and bottle washer who served in the last war even in the regulars or the volunteers rushed to

---

[54] Eastwood, BJ., Lt. Col."Early Days" Regiment Journal Vol. 1 No. 1 p. 7

join."[55]Unfortunately while these men filled the ranks of the army the officer corps met with a slightly worse fate. Customs and Immigration officers, bank clerks and salesman and a large number of ex-civil servants were given temporary short service commissions of five to seven years duration. They all received only the barest minimum of training and at that state "a period spent in the Cadet Force was considered the ultimate qualification."[56] Indeed the Cadet Force would go on in the future to contribute to the protection of the country during the 1990 jihadist coup attempt. In general the Short Service officers training was of four to six weeks duration to up to three months either in Canada or England. In most of the cases this was the total extent of training they received in addition to one or two secondments to base units abroad for one to two weeks.

At the army's inception the plan as it was laid out was that while the newly recruited officer cadets were sent off to the military academies to be trained as young professionals, to take over command, the temporary short service officers would hold on before stepping down at the end of their contracts. The objective therefore was to have the uniformed presence of indigenous 'officers' complementing the members of seconded personnel until the return to base of the smartly trained young men, selected to lead the country's Defence Force. The aim of this plan was to have a totally professional officer corps in nucleus and by

____

[55] Kelshall, GTM. Lt., Ten Days In April p.26

[56] ibid

virtue of leadership and training imparted by these young professionals, a totally professional army at the end of six to seven years when the short service officers, selected to 'hold the fort' while the cadets were training, would have been phased out. When this time arrived the temporary short service officers were advisors to the ministry (as senior officers) and they would hardly have advised phasing themselves out. Given the power which a military officer holds within a military unit or environment compared to that of a civil servant, bank clerk or salesman this was not a realistic expectation.

Another reason why the senior officers were not phased out was as a result of a distrust of youth. Militaries the world over are comprised of young eager 19-24 year old officer cadets and midshipmen. It is a part of the very tradition of military life. Since the local officer corps was comprised mostly of ex-civil servants and the body responsible for determining policy. A civil service ministry where there was not even a Ministry of Defence but a shared Ministry of Home Affairs, and not a single military specialist who understood how a military should be run, it must be understood that the prevailing attitude within and about how the military should be run was that of a civil servant's perception.[57] Burnham and Ghust (1979) actually state that "Before everything else the military officer is a public servant"[58]

The short service officers did not have the benefit of a long period of military training that would have removed these non-professional attitudes. The dominant belief that the senior officers cultivated then was that only with age should responsibility come, thus convoluting the very essence of all militaries. This is the exact opposite of the way the military runs. In the civil service a person has to achieve a certain age before they became eligible for any responsibility. There is an absolute distrust in youth evidenced by the now ingrained slogan 'experience necessary'. In the military on the other hand it was the young newly trained officers who held immediate responsibility for those subordinate to them. This was of course justified by the fact that a typical professionally trained rounded officer would have spent something close to two to three years in training at various elite military institutions. The young military officer fresh from receiving a commission is at a peak in terms of their professional capabilities. Their leadership theory is firmly grounded and experience in the form of continuous active duty and compulsive residence on the base. They are continually exposed to situations which polish off their competence in their chosen skill, officer-ship. The local young officers were viewed

---

[57] Burnham and Ghust 1979 UWI Public Administration Diploma Thesis pg34-37

[58] IBID

with utter contempt by their older, senior short service officers. Frequently the only defence against youth and the knowledge of youth and its abilities was the very power the senior officers clutched and exercised ruthlessly in cutting down the young officers.

The extensions of the senior short service officers contracts entrenched them into the system, securing them privileges not even the young professionals would be entitled to. Because a great majority of the officers transferred from the civil service occupation including the Customs and Immigration Service they were promised no loss of seniority and given the same retirement age that they would have had, had they remained in their original service. Invariably this age was sixty. The retirement age for the professional officers was forty-seven, depending on the rank they attained. The extension therefore meant that in all likelihood, extension after extension would be granted leaving the short service officers in post -who chose to remain in the service-long after the professional officers had retired. This was contrary to the terms the cadets were recruited under and when the first extensions were granted a promotional bottleneck was created whereby the young professionally trained officers could not be promoted because the short service officers monopolized all the vacancies. The extension of contracts therefore meant that the young officers would have to wait for up to six to ten years before being promoted to their level of competency which could not be done, because the rank structure was filled with officers who were improperly trained, and for all their good qualities and devotion to service for the country incompetent.

The officer corps in 1962 was seventeen strong. There were slots for one Lieutenant Colonel to command, the unit (a Battalion is commanded by a Lieutenant Colonel and a Battalion comprises 700 to 800 men), three Majors, five Captains and eight Lieutenants. Seven of these were British seconded officers, three majors and four captains and Lt. Colonel Pearce Gould. By December 1963 there were twenty0nine officers in the service, twelve Lieutenants, eight Captains, eight Majors and a Lieutenant Colonel. In 1969, the administrative structure catered for seven Majors and eight Captains. The number of professionally trained young officers were twelve Sandhurst and three Mons trained and within the structure the professional officers held one Major slot out of seven slots and three junior Captains slots out of eight available. The seconded personnel had all returned to Britain in 1964 and a local officer was left in command, after a handover from Joffre Serrette to Lt. Colonel Stanley Johnson. Of the fifteen trained young men, five had more continuous military service and training then all the short service officers. The Short service officers had functioned under the protection of the seconded personnel but on their departure, the cloak of competence was lifted. These officers showed very little interest in or capacity for leadership but became concerned with authority and status to an almost unbearable level. They were concerned only with the image of being officers.[59] This was the basic situation that existed in the Regiment prior to 1970. As is clearly evidenced, these problems manifested themselves over the years but the clear

---

[59] Spencer, J. Maj., Problems, Pitfalls and Possibilities. P2

source was in the manner in which the Regiment was established and the perception that existed in the ministry about the military.

CHAPTER TWELVE: TRINIDAD AND TOBAGO COAST GUARD

The Coast Guard was officially formed on August 27, 1962. It comprised almost in entirety, serving members of the Marine Branch Police detachment. At inception, the unit had six officers and forty-two men with four launches.

Sea Sprite

Sea Hawk

Sea Scout

Sea Bee

Thirty-nine of the forty-two men came from the Police Service and the founder officers were the British Commander Loftus Peyton Jones, DSO, DSC and Bar; Lt. Cmdr. D. Bloom, GM of the Police Branch; Lt. M.O. Williams; Lt. P. Ramdhanie, Lt. J. Wilson and S/Lt. J. Mader. Two officer cadets intended to be the first local professional military officers George Arnold and Richard Kelshall were recruited and sent to Britannia Royal Naval College, Dartmouth, UK in Sept 1963 to be trained by the Royal Navy. Three short service officers attended a two month Divisional Officer's course in Portsmouth in February 1963 so that some semblance of military bearing and discipline would inform the local short service temporary element of the unit prior to the return of the officer cadets from the Royal Naval College. In

November of 1963, thirty-three recruit ratings were taken in. In November of 1962, another British officer, Lt. Cmdr. L. Goldstraw came on strength and in December, Lr. Cmdr. Favell joined as Engineer Officer. Apart from these British officers, six Chiefs and Petty Officers also came from the Royal Navy with Varying terms of engagement, two of them remaining till the end of 1970.

 Because the unit was comprised of former serving police men and its executive officer, Lt. Cmdr. Bloom, an active serving member of a marine unit, the Coast Guard managed to establish very close links with the Police Service. This was something the army was unable to do because the army's existence was in fact a rival body to the Police. At that time the Police maintained the 'role' of the army and was virtually equivalent to the army – this 'role' of theirs was thus disbanded with the establishment of the Regiment. In the absence of a regular military element prior to Independence, the Police were trained almost to the point of military professionalism. Lt. Cmdr. Bloom was an Englishman who became a citizen of Trinidad and Tobago and joined the Police Service. He was later the first Trinidadian to command the Coast Guard. In 1963, the Coast Guard was called into action when hurricane Flora hit Tobago. It was responsible for carrying medical supplies and food and other relief items to Tobago. In 1965, the first two naval fast patrol boats arrived in Trinidad the 'Trinity' and the 'Courland Bay'. The ships were brought across the Atlantic by the members of the Trinidad and Tobago Coast Guard in entirety under the Command of David Bloom. In 1966, the Air Wing of the Coast Guard was inaugurated and the two pilots of the Trinidad and Tobago Coast Guard Air Wing flew the brand new Cessna 337 Skymaster from the United States to its new base at Piarco. Another hurricane, Alma, again required the services of the Coast Guard. By 1968, the Coast Guard had exercised success fully with both the United States Navy and the Royal Navy and carried out numerous search and rescue missions.

The role of the Coast Guard then was summed up as: -

Fisheries Protection

Anti-smuggling

Aid to Civil Power

Search and Rescue

By 1968, there were fourteen officers and sixty-seven other ranks. There was one midshipman, three Sub Lieutenants, six Lieutenants and three Lieutenants and three Lieutenant Commanders, Williams, Goldstraw and the Supply Officer Conrad Hutchinson. Sub Lieutenant Mader had transferred to the regiment in 1964, Lt. Ramdhanie retired in 1966 and the first Supply Officer, Lt. Wilson had retired in 1963. The return of Tim Favell to England in 1964 also opened the way for a local engineer, Arnold Neckles. The retirement of the founder members of the officer corps, all except one, kept the promotional channels open to allow the newly trained cadets and midshipmen to assume roles where they felt they were making a contribution at their level of competence.

In the same period of time that the Coast Guard accomplished its expansion and participated in Search and Rescue missions and exercised with two world navies, the Regiment was called out not only twice in the eight years in between their inception and the mutiny apart from two or three exercises in conjunction with the police and the American armed forces.

Having examined the inception of the Coast Guard let us now look at the question of leadership.

In the army when the seconded men left, the middle and upper levels of the officer corps were short service, recruited, and essentially lesser trained men than the ones they led. In the Coast Guard Lt. Cdr. Goldstraw was the Executive Officer until 1971 and above this was an ex British Merchant Navy Officer, life-long sailor and maritime domain leader, Cdr. David Bloom. This type of consistent leadership was absent in the regiment. Within the ranks of the sailors-as well as the non-commissioned officers - were a stalwart from which the ratings gained their professionalism. There was therefore no time for the officers and sailors to rest upon their rank and status. The Coast Guard was constantly at work. The stature of the leadership in the officer corps was an important factor in the stability of the Coast Guard. The leadership qualities of individual officers within the Coast Guard was tested daily because the Coast Guard was virtually constantly at war with its enemies: the elements and the sea. The sea is such that it demands only the most competent and alert professionals to successfully carry out tasks, or to survive at all during long periods. The sea, weeds out the poor leaders and the incompetents. One cannot fight with the great unknown of the

109

sea daily facing numerous and diverse challenges each time one goes to work without becoming a skilled technician in the domain by force. Proficiency at sea invariably lends itself to the task of motivator and leader, to those under an officer's command. The Coast Guard officer therefore and the Coast Guard sailor is constantly proving oneself both to the sea and to those with whom they work. A naval officer was either sharp and professional or given shore assignment. Each time an officer went to sea invariably they were responsible for the safekeeping of million-dollar assets and the lives of their crew. The soldier on the other hand had to wait on a war or natural disaster which might have required the service of the army. A soldier therefore was not tested constantly, and the mettle of the officer was always in debate until proven. The sailors and officers of the Coast Guard were busy and were happy, doing what they had signed up to do – to go to sea. They also had the equipment necessary. Had this been different then the Coast Guard may well have joined instead of stopping the mutiny of 1970.

SECTION VI :
THE PATH TO APRIL 21ST

CHAPTER THIRTEEN:

REASONS FOR THE BREAKDOWN OF RELATIONS BETWEEN THE MINISTRY AND THE MILITARY IN 1970

When asked the reason why things ran so smoothly for the first six years, Maj. J. Spencer (Ret'd), replied that there were four reasons for this:-

a) The newness of the organization and the originality of the idea of being soldiers and in some cases being soldiers again and reunited with old war buddies.

b) The work involved in actually building the unit demanded the attention of all the soldiers, both officers and men. There was a considerable amount of training which had to be done by the first batch of enlisted men, as a new recruits came into the service.

c)The four recruit intakes as mentioned above occupied most of the six years since intakes were brought in 1962, 1963, 1964 and 1966. In addition to this young officers were in and out of the unit at a rapid rate being trained abroad.

d) The withdrawal of the seconded personnel in 1964 meant even more work for the unit since they were no longer being protected by experience. In addition to this the novelty of a local commander excited the unit.

By the same token Maj. Spencer intimates that this last factor signaled the decline of the unit. This was not because the locals were incapable of doing the job but because of the apparent unsuitability of some of the locals into whose hands the responsibility passed." [60]

The short term officers. With the further handover of power to Lt. Col Stanley Johnson in 1968 there was suddenly an unmistakable decline in standards of discipline and morale in the unit. [61] It was simply a question, according to Maj. Spencer of the wrong people selected to do the job and not a reflection on their personal standards of loyalty or interests or goodwill."[62]

The extension of contracts in 1968 and in 1969 ensured that the slide in discipline would continue since the middle level officers did not know how to contain it and the lower level junior officers did not choose to help and in fact participated and encouraged the activities. Their chances of promotion and recognition of their professional ability were virtually swept away or ignored and in fact there was an incident on two occasions and when a Coast Guard lieutenant in charge of the Coast Guard Internal Security Platoon and an army second Lieutenant were teaching alternative combat tactics to individuals under their command and a senior short service officer berated them in front of their

---

[60] Spencer, J. Maj. Problems, Pitfalls, Possibilities pg. 15

[61] Spencer, J. Maj. Problems, Pitfalls, Possibilities pg. 15

[62] Ibid pg.16

113

units for teaching them rubbish, that simply did not exist because he, the senior officer had never heard of them.[63]

As the year 1970 rolled around the junior officers had grown accustomed to gritting their teeth and biding their time, till their opportunity to do their job arose.[64] Soon, leadership at the very highest levels, a lack of experience in actual combat and emergency conditions (which would have kept the soldiers occupied), limited knowledge, inefficiency and power playing inherited from the civil service where many of the short service officers originated left the young semi-professional regiment totally without direction. The situation with the ministry also did not help the crisis that was building. The lines of communications slowly became more and more blocked and on several occasions commanding officers of both units were made to wait for days before gaining access to their minister to discuss supposedly urgent matters.[65] The result of such treatment and the low profile status afforded the military resulted in the creation of a military mentality that held sacred the belief that the ministry was itself a cumbersome inefficient bureaucracy. In fact the ministry literally knew nothing about how to treat the military so far as the accusation was concerned it was probably true due to the absence of military specialists or advisors in the ministry

---

[63] Kelshall, GTM. Lt., Ten Days in April

[64] Kelshall, GTM. Lt., Ten Days In April

[65] Author interviews

which by the time 1970 had rolled around had very little attention to focus on the military; bearing in mind that it was responsible for Home Affairs; and 1970 certainly brought with it crisis after crisis in the form of the black power uprisings. The physical distance of the military (out of sight/out of mind) took on greater dimensions in the eyes of the public servants staffing the ministry. My belief is that had there been in existence a separate ministry of Defence which was staffed with military advisors and whose concern was matters dealing with the civilian-military relationship, this situation could have been avoided (1970) or at least the problems inherited at the regiment's inception, better understood and dealt with.

CHAPTER FOURTEEN: THE APRIL UPRISING

In 1968 after the change in command from Serrette to Johnson a large number of non-commissioned officers refused to re-engage on completion of their contracts (in direct contrast to their senior officers). Quite a few of the younger non-commissioned officers also relinquished their contracts and resigned. "They could not identify the cause of their disillusionment and were just fed up and not happy with the way things were going." [66]Among the younger ranks the feelings of frustration and boredom were no less intense and "the danger signals had been flashing for some time before the final explosion." [67]   Large numbers of men reported sick daily.

An increase in the number of men reporting sick should have told an alert Commanding Officer that morale in the unit was at an ebb. The conditions outside of the army with increasing civil unrest, bus strikes and mass gatherings and violence undoubtedly influenced the increasing unrest within the barracks. "An army recruited from among the very people to whom the principal addresses were being made could not have

---

[66] Spencer, J. Maj.   Ibid   P. 18

[67] IBID P 19

116

been expected to be uninfluenced by what was taking place in the country."[68]

On the 21st of April due to high incidents of arson and violence a state of emergency was called. Three officers in the army under surveillance for insubordination to their senior officers were being separated due to the escalating unrest. When announcement of their new posting, Lt. Lasalle to the Coast Guard, Lt. Shah to the Police and Lt. Bazie to Tobago the three officers spontaneously and without a plan mutinied and refused to leave the base. Lt's Shah and Lasalle attempted to arrest Maj. Christopher and Capt. Spencer, but were overpowered and locked up. When news of their imprisonment reached the men under them and by who they were well loved, a mass attempt was made to free them and a state of confusion ensued. The Coast Guard was informed and attempted to quell the chaos by shelling Teteron Bay from the sea under the command of Lt. M. Williams, this action proved useless and the Trinity returned to the Staubles Bay where Lt. Williams disembarked and the second in command S/Lt. Richard Kelshall subsequently took the vessel back to sea and attempted to shell the roadside when a convoy of soldiers made an attempt to march to Port of Spain. Loyalist troops assembled outside of the main gate at Teteron under the command of Capt. Spencer in the puzzling absence of Col Johnson. On the 23rd of April the previous Commanding Officer of the army Lt. Col. Joffre Serrette was recalled from retirement to take

---

[68] IBID P23

control of the situation. On May 1st the mutineer troops surrendered and the mutineers arrested and charged for Treason. By July 1972 all of the mutineers were released on the recommendation of the Attorney General due to a series of bungled attempts in the court room by judges and lawyers alike. So ended the Mutiny of 1970 with the person who faced and serve two years imprisonment among the largest sentences served by the mutineers being Lt. David Brizan who was not even in Trinidad when the Regiment junior officers mutinied but had written a letter to one of the mutineers voicing his support and agreeing with the cause in the event that such a thing should occur.

CHAPTER FIFTEEN: THE POST MUTINY DEFENCE FORCE

After 1970, the loyal soldiers lived through a virtual hell. Up to 1974 there was no statement policy from the government on the failure of the unit. This fact which is really most astounding, coupled with a situation where the structure and leadership of the Regiment remained unchanged and in fact identical to prior to the mutiny, had a devastating effect on the morale of the remaining soldiers. The mutineers had stated publicly why they mutinied and the government never made any attempt to rectify the situation, in fact, the only policy which came down from the ministry appeared to be to try and forget about the mutiny as quickly as possible. The Marcano Committee was ordered to sit in the week after the mutiny to ascertain why the mutiny occurred. Up to today the report submitted at the end of the week has never seen the light of day, nor any action in any form taken to implement its recommendations. In May 1970, yet another committee, called the Moore Committee, sat. Its objective was to report on the role, scope and functions of the Defence Force. Twenty years later that report too has never been seen or heard from. Both reports were submitted to the ministry for its action and clearly any inaction on the part of the government certainly was not from a lack of information on the matter. The army spent four years in limbo with absolutely no policy directives being given except for the reassurance by the government finally in 1977 that it would not be disbanded. Apparently not even a

119

mutiny a most extreme and disturbing occurrence in any other military could have changed the unjust situation that existed. Lasalle, Shah and Bazie were not mad men, nor were they bad officers, in fact, they were some of the most brilliant officer material the Regiment has seen then or since. The unfortunate thing was, they were just better soldiers than their superiors. During the term of office of Lt. Colonel Serrette after the mutiny, ten of the professionally trained young officers resigned their commissions in bewilderment and frustration. Only two officers retired. Within two years of Serrette's own final retirement, eight of the short service senior officers retired or left the force. These figures show that the absolute opposite of the demands of the mutineers was carried out. Since official policy stated that the mutiny should be forgotten, the situation arose where the senior officers of the regiment were apparently protected from the consequences of their incompetence and they sat back believing they were the victims of poor quality junior officers. In this period after the mutiny, three hundred soldiers left the army in disbelief that the rank structure over which a mutiny occurred could remain unchanged and the military still obviously viewed with a lack of concern. The only thing to come out of the mutiny was the increased power of the Police Force. All of the army's hard machinery were seized and sent to them. At the end of the decade, the Trinidad and Tobago Regiment acquired seven Lieutenant Colonels. No longer did that rank signify the military command of a battalion (700 to 800 men) but instead in became a badge of long service. Only one of these men promoted, played any part in the front line of stopping the mutiny. "The system that the mutineers tried to change by sacrificing their own careers had apparently not only fed on the mutiny but grew to undreamed of proportions that were unimaginable in the minds of the professional officers". [69]

In 1970, some of the best, most professional soldiers in the Regiment mutinied, opposing them on the land were the remainder of the competent professionals. The older, middle order officers quietly slipped into the background" and eventually got promoted for doing just that. [70]

In the Coast Guard, the' loyal unit' between 1970 and 1980 one officer was promoted, one was permanently transferred, seven retired and sixteen resigned. An additional five engineer officers left the Coast Guard by 1980 bringing the total loss of strength to twenty eight. [71]

In total, twenty-three officers were lost and in the regiment twelve left. The question asked by many was which unit had really mutinied. The Coast Guard was never thanked as a unit for remaining loyal. Individual officers (2) received awards but for saving the country – The Coast Guard was rewarded by the promotion of seven Colonels in the Regiment and nothing even near that to correspond in their unit. The Regiment apparently

---

[69] Kelshall GTM. Lt., Ten Days In April P. 236

[70] Kelshall, GTM Ten days in April

[71] The Guardian, 25 January 1987 front page

was being rewarded for the mutiny whilst the Coast Guard was virtually ignored.

If there was a breakdown in civil military relations in 1970, the situation appeared to have worsened after the mutiny. The loss of communication with the ministry was never repaired and only now in 1990 does there appear to be any sense of understanding on the ministry's part toward the military. In 1989, Lt. Colonel Theodore was made military advisor to the Minister of National Security before becoming Chief of Defence Staff. Clearly, this is or was a step (since the post is now vacant once again) in the right direction, however any army officer is fit only to advise on the army and a naval officer on the navy. The two units are radically different and founded in totally separate traditions, skills, training and discipline. Perhaps in the near future this will be recognized and rectified.

Today, the role of the Coast Guard was expanded to unbelievable dimensions (see Appendix) but the Army's role has remained essentially the same. A more diversified, more meaningful role in terms of social integration is yet to be enunciated by the relevant authorities.

CHAPTER SIXTEEN: CONCLUSION

There are five motives for mutiny: nationalist, institutional, ethnic, class and personalist. The events of 1970 occurred not because of class or nationalist motives but because of predominantly institutional reasons. Ethical motives were clearly an influence on the rank and file of the Regiment as evidenced by the fact that the original plotters reported that there was a vague intention to meet up with a black power rally, which did not come to pass.[72] The three officers who led the insurrection were of different ethnic backgrounds in that Lt. Lasalle was mixed race, Lt. Shah was Indian and Lt. Bazie was black.

The reaction of the soldiers to the actions of the three young officers was spontaneous and agitated as a result of the upheavals in society caused by the black power movement because most of the soldiers were black. A state of Emergency had been declared in Port of Spain and prior to the insurrection, army patrols were due to leave to go into the town to maintain order.

The soldiers who did join in the mutiny were not joining a revolt in the army based on black power grievances, though this did feed into the heightened senses of all the participants at the time.

---

[72] Burkett, C. Reflections of a soldier 2009 pp148-9

123

This is obvious because the command of the army was black and the ministry above the Commanding Officer also staffed with black civil servants led by Eric Williams the black scholar who was head of the Government. Additionally there was a greater number of white officers with commissions in the Coast Guard and while there had been an official enquiry into heightened racism tensions in the Coast Guard conducted by Ron Cuffy, there had been no mutiny in that arm of the Defence Force.[73]   There was never any official outcome recorded of the enquiry due to the outbreak of events in Teteron the Barracks of the Regiment.

In addition, the possibility that the ethnic motive influenced the rank and file of the army to mutiny in an attempt at protest directed at the white minister of Home Affairs Mr. Montano is very slim. There was virtually no contact with the Minister.

A Minister and his/her policy is far removed from the life of an ordinary sailor or soldier. Few soldiers would probably even have met their minister.

A soldier's interest tends to be focused on his/her platoon and company commanders, since it is these people who have most direct influence in the lives of their platoons and companies.

A further condition singled out was a belief that there was a marked dissimilarity in the conditions of service in similar ranks

---

[73] Interview Adm. R Kelshall then Lt., on February 21 2011 and interview Capt Louis Le Gendre 18 Feb 1989

between local ranks and seconded foreign ranks manifested in different food, quarters and pay which the seconded personnel received.[74]

The question of personalist intervention is perhaps only marginal in that the officers in one of their demands asked to be promoted to Captain. This does reflect personal ambition but is more easily explained if considered an institutional motive.

If we recall that mutinies based on institutional interests have to do with civilian interference in the professionalism of the army, threats in general to the professional autonomy of the army and interference by civilians in determining the standards of leadership within the army; then without question, we can see that then reason for the insurrection in 1970 was predominantly institutionally based.

In fact we can clearly see it as a direct result of the method of establishment of the force. The inception of the Defence Force was a feature of Independence. Additional contributing factors include a limited or lack of a suitable role for the army. They were exasperated by an indifference by the ministry to the military. This is clearly evidenced by an ill-defined paradigm of civil military relations.

---

[74] The Defence Force from Inception to 1974 Syndicate 2 Officers Staff Paper and study day page 5

Part of this latter reason is also to be discerned in an increased indifference to Lt. Colonels Serrette and Johnson when Lt Col Pierce Gould handed over command.

This has been attributed to the remnants of colonial mentality by the ministry toward the 'black' commanding officers of the Regiment. [75]

All of these grievances went toward the spontaneous decision to mutiny by the young officers due to build up of frustrations that were work related. As Finer (1957) states "Motives provide a necessary but not sufficient condition for intervention. To move the military to act, these motives have to be catalysed into an emotion" and that pent up emotion must find opportunity. [76]Such was presented on the morning of April 21st .1970.

There was also the fact that as the Ministry did not understand the military it attempted to run it like another arm of the civil service.

From inception to Mutiny and indeed beyond, the ministry was staffed by civil servants with very little understanding of the mechanics of the military. "A military Service cannot be an

____

[75] The Defence Force from Inception to 1974 Syndicate 2 Officers Staff Paper and study day page 3

[76] Finer, S. E. (1988). *The Man on Horseback: The Role of the Military in Politics.* Boulder, Colorado: Westview Press. Pp63

126

extension of the Civil Service, either in thought or deed." [77] Perhaps, of all the factors identified in this book this was the single greatest contributory fact to the activities which occurred during those ten days in April when the shape of Civil Military Relations in Trinidad and Tobago were forever reshaped.

---

[77] Kelshall , GTM Ten Days in April pp18

INTERVIEWS

Ministry of National Security. March 29, 1990

Ms. Vicky Carrington: Head of Defence AO 5

Ms. Annette Nathaniel: Head of Defense AO 2

Trinidad and Tobago Coast Guard

Lt. Tony Roach 15 April, 1990

Lt. Noel Penco 17 April, 1990

Lt. G.T.M. Kelshall 11, 15, 19 April, 1990 – Military Historian

Cdr. R.W.R. Kelshall 9, 11, 15, 17 April 1990 – COGS

Lt. Cdr. B.H.M Brash 10 April, 1990

Cdr. Jack Williams 17 April, 1990 – Ex COCG

Trinidad and Tobago Regiment.

Maj. D. Williams – PRO, Office of Chief of Defence Staff   9, 12, 17, 21 April, 1990

Lt. Col. R.N. Brown – CO TTR 20 March, 1989

Col. J.L. Theodore – Vice CDS, Military Advisor to Ministry, 20, March 1989

Maj. J.A. Spencer 26 March, 1989

128

Capt. Louis Legendre 18 February, 1989

Gerard Montano 18 February, 1989

APPENDIX A

ACT ESTABLISHING THE TRINIDAD AND TOBAGO DEFENCE FORCE

1st Session First Legislature Trinidad and Tobago II Elizabeth

TRINIDAD AND TOBAGO

ACT NO. 7 OF 1962

AN ACT to provide for the defence of Trinidad and Tobago by the establishment of a Trinidad and Tobago Defence Force and to provide for matters connected therewith and incidental thereto.

Assented to 22nd August, 1962

BE IT ENACTED by the Queen's Most Excellent Majesty, by and with the advice and consent of the senate and House of Representatives of Trinidad and Tobago, and by the authority of the same, as follows:-

PART I

Preliminary

1.   (1)   This Act may be cited as the Defence Act, 1962

      (2)   This Act has effect from the 1st day of June, 1962

5.   (1)   There shall be established and maintained in the Territory a body of military forces styled "the Trinidad and Tobago Defence Force" consisting of –

(a)   a unit of land forces;

(b)   a coast guard; and

(c)   such other units as the Governor may from time to time think fit to be formed, and styled by such designation as the Governor shall declare by notice published in the Royal Gazette.

(2)   Every unit shall be charged with the defence of the time Territory and with such other duties as may from time to time be defined by the Minister.

(3)   The Governor may at any time order that any unit or part thereof shall be employed out of or beyond the Territory.

(4)   The Minister may order that any officer or other rank shall proceed to any place outside the Territory for the purpose of undergoing instruction or training or for duty or employment.

Several amendments were made, the most significant being Act No. 32 of 1979.

APPENDIX B

Role of the Coast Guard

The role of the Coast Guard since its formation in August 1962 has been broadly interpreted as:

"contribution to the preservation of national security, providing assistance to the land forces and, maintaining a search and rescue capability".

The role of the coast Guard as it has evolved can be broken down into the following missions:

preserve the security of the nation's coastline and the territorial sea. This entails the following duties:

coastal surveillance and sovereignty patrols;

anti-terrorist activities;

anti-smuggling patrols narcotics, weapons, illegal immigrants; and

the provision of logistic, amphibious and tactical support for the land forces

to provide a search and rescue service as agreed to under the international treaty and convention to meet:

the ICAO requirement;

the IMO requirement; and,

national needs.

to safeguard and preserve the national marine resources locate in territorial waters and the EEZ by:

the patrol and protection of offshore petro-chemical facilities and resources;

the protection and preservation of the nation's fishery resources;

to implement anti-pollution and pollution control measures; and,

to monitor the presence of safe navigation practices in national waters through the Harbour Master's Ordnance, the Pleasure Boat Act, and through vessel traffic.

to provide assistance to the following agencies with marine responsibilities:

Customs;

Police;

Ministry of Health;

Prison Service;

Marine Scientific Organizations; and,

Liaison with visiting navies.

133

to detect and/or counter a hostile naval threat of action by a foreign power either unilaterally of in concert with allied forces; render aid to civil authorities.

BIBLIOGRAPHY

Andreski, S. 1954, *Military organization and society*, Routledge & Kegan Paul, London

Arlirptor, B & Baker P (eds) 1986, *African Armies: Evolution and Capabilities*, WestView Press, Colorado.

Arlinghaus, B. E. 1984, Military *development in Africa: the political and economic risks of arms transfers.* Westview Press Boulder, Colorado.

Baker, D 1981, *Soldiering On,* Deutsch, London.

Ball, A. R. 1971, *Modern politics and government.* Macmillan London

Baylis, J. 1946-, (ed.) & Wirtz, James J., 1958-, (ed.) & Gray, Colin S., (ed) 2016, *Strategy in the contemporary world: an introduction to strategic studies*, 5th edition, Oxford Oxford University Press

Baynes. JC 1972, *The Soldier in Modern Society*, Eyre Methuen, London.

Bozzoli, C, Brück, T. 2010, Determinants of Protests: Longitudinal Evidence from Ukraine's Orange Revolution. *MICROCON,* Research Working Paper 30.

Burkett, C. (2009). Reflections of a Soldier. Port Of Spain: CARB.

Caribbean Studies Association Conference. (1987). *The*

135

challenge of change: leadership in the Caribbean: Caribbean Studies Association XII International Congress, Belize City, Belize, May 27-29, 1987.

Cock, J & Olive, R 1984, *War, State and Society*, Macmillan, London.

Command of the Defence Council, Revised 1967, *The Queen's Regulations of the Royal Navy*, Her Majesty Stationery Office, London.

Corbett, C 1973, *The Latin American Military as a Social Political Force: Bolivia/Argentina*, University of Miami, Miami.

Corvisier, A 1979, *Armies and Societies in Europe: 1494–1789*, Indiana Union Press, London.

Cowley, R & Parker, G 2001, *The Readers Companion to Military History*, Mariner Books, Boston.

Cushing, HA (ed) 1907, *The writings of Samuel Adams*, Putnam, New York.

Debray, R 1967, *Revolution in the Revolution*, Grove Press Inc, New York.

Deutsche, K 1988, *Analysis of International Relations*, 3rd edn, Prentice-Hall International, London.

Derrick, SRE 1974, *The Role of the Defence Force in the Development of Trinidad and Tobago*, Staff Paper, Teteron Barracks.

Doorn, J A A van. 1969, *Military profession and military regimes. Commitments and conflicts*, Mouton The Hague

Dowse, R. E. 1969, "The Military and Political Development" in C. Leys (ed), *Politics and change in developing countries: studies in the theory and practice of development*, pp. 213-246. Cambridge U.P London

Eccles, H. E. 1965, *Military concepts and philosophy*, Rutgers University Press, New Brunswick, N.J

Edwards, Stewart. 1982, *Lengthening shadows: Birth and revolt of the Trinidad army.* Inprint Caribbean Trinidad

Ellis, M. 1885, *The History of the First West India Regiment.* Crystal Palace Press, London.

Finer, S. E. 1974, *Comparative government*, Penguin, Harmondsworth, Middlesex

Finer, SE, 1988. *The Man on Horseback: The Role of the Military in Politics*, Boulder, Westview Press, Colorado.

Galbraith, J. K. 1969, *How to control the military*, Harper's, New York,

Graham, J.J. (trans) 1991, *On War*, by General Clausewitz, Dorset Press, Dorchester.

Guardian, T. T, 1987, January 25, *The destruction of the Coast Guard*, pp. 1.

Harries – Jenkins and Van Doorn. 1976,"The Military
and the Problems of Legitimacy." in *Studies
in International Society* Sage Publishers, California.

Huntington, S. 1957, *The Soldier and The State: The Theory
and Politics of Civil-Military Relations*, Belknap Press of
Harvard University Press, Cambridge.

Janowitz, M. 1964, *The Military in the Political Development
of Nations,* University of Chicago Press, Chicago.

Johnson, J (ed) 1962, *Role of Military in Underdeveloped
Countries*, Princeton University
Press.

Kelshall, C. 1989. *Military in Developing Nations. An
examination of the Trinidad and Tobago Defence Force and
its peacetime potential.* Unpublished

Kelshall, C. 1995. 'Mutiny or Revolution' in Ryan, S. D. &
Stewart, T. (eds) 1995, *The Black Power Revolution of
1970: a retrospective*, I.S.E.R., pp. 419-440. University of
the West Indies, St. Augustine, Trinidad

Kelshall, C. 2010, *Revolution or Mutiny: Trinidad and
Tobago Regiment in the 1970 Military Crisis.* Antitype
Press, London.

Kelshall C. M. 2013, *Revolution or Mutiny. The Military
as a Pressure Group*, LAP LAMBERT Academic Publishing

Kelshall, GTM 1987, *Ten Days in April: 1970 Regiment
Revolution and the Role of the Coast Guard*. Unpublished.

Kelshall, GTM 1989, *The First Coast Guardsmen*, Unpublished.

Kelshall, R. 1980, An *Administrative Study of the Trinidad
and Tobago Coast Guard 1980 – 1988: Organization Role
Requirement and Future*, MOM. DFHQ.

Lee, J. M. 1969 *African Armies and Civil Order*, Praeger, New York.

Lider, J. 1983. *Military theory: concept, structure,*

problems. Aldershot, Hants, Eng, Gower.

Loveman, B, Davies, T (eds), 1997, *The Politics of Antipolitics,*

SR Books, New York.

Lyons, G 1965, *Schools for Strategy*, Praeger, New York.

Mashshat, `Abd al-Mun`im. 1985, National *security in the
Third World.* Westview Press Boulder

Ministry of National Security Trinidad and Tobago. 1978.

*Report of Cabinet Appointed Team of Officials on Mechanics
of Implementing a Program of Academic Training for
Defence Force Personnel.*

Morris, C 1983, *The United States-Caribbean basin
military connection: a perspective on regional military-to-
military relationships,* American Enterprise Institute for
Public Policy Research, Washington, D.C.

National Security Document 44/5/2. *Establishment
and Administration of the Trinidad and Tobago Defence
Force.* The Government of Trinidad and Tobago.
Unpublished

Owens, M 1986, 'American Strategic Culture and Civil
Military Relations: The Case of JCS
Reform', *Naval War College Review*, vol. 39, no. 2, Naval
War College Press, Newport R. I. U.S.A

Oxaal, F 1971, *Race and Revolutionary Consciousness.
An existential report on the 1970 Black
Power Revolt in Trinidad*, Schenkman Books, Cambridge
Mass.

Payne, S. G. 1980, *Fascism: Comparison and Definition*,
University of Wisconsin, Madison.

Pye, L 1971 "Armies in the process of political modernization
" In Finicle and Gable *Readings in Political Development.*
Thomas Wiley Publication. NY

Perlmutter, A 1969, 'The Praetorian State and the
Praetorian Army: Toward a Taxonomy of Civil-Military
Relations in Developing Polities', Comparative Politics,
vol. 1, no. 3, pp. 382-404.

Putman, R 1967, 'Towards Expanding Military Intervention
in Latin America Politics', *World Politics*, vol. 20 no. 1, 83-
110, DOI: 10.2307/2009729

Ryan, S. D. & Stewart, T. 1995, *The Black Power Revolution of*

1970: a retrospective, I.S.E.R., University of the West Indies, St. Augustine, Trinidad

Sctiellers, T. 1966, *Arms and Influence,* Yale University Press, New Haven & London.

Shah, R. L. 1995, 'Reflections on the Mutiny and Trial' in Ryan & Stewart, *The Black Power Revolution: A Retrospective*, pp. 509-522. Institute of Social and Economic Research, Port of Spain.

Slater, R 1968, *With Sword and Plow: Role of American Military in Contemporary Society*, Praeger, New York.

Spencer, J 1974, *Problems Pitfalls Possibilities. An analytical study of the Military in Trinidad and Tobago.* University of the West Indies, Chaguaramas.

Spencer, J 1987, *The Military in Trinidad and Tobago*, Staff Paper, Trinidad.

Spiers, E 1980, *The Army and Society, 1815-1914,* Longman, London.

Steeple, M 1982, *The Trinidad and Tobago Regiment,* Trinidad and Tobago Joint Services Staff College Pamphlet

Stepan, A 1971, *The Military in Politics,* Princeton University Press, Princeton.

Syndicate, II 1974, *The Defence Force from Inception to TTDF*, Officers study day presentation.

Trinidad and Tobago Regiment 1967 *Journal of the Trinidad and Tobago Regiment.*   Vol 1 No1 1962 – Vol No. 10 1967

Trinidad and Tobago Coast Guard 1962-1989 *The Mariner: The Journal of the Trinidad and Tobago Coast Guard* Trinidad and Tobago

Trinidad and Tobago Government Defence Act, Act No. 7 1962, Act No. 9 1962 – 1963, Act No. 1979

Vagts, A 1959., *A history of militarism: [civilian and military,* Rev. ed], Meridian Books, New York

Welch, C 1967, Soldier and State in Africa, *The Journal of Modern African Studies,* vol. 5 no. 3, 305-322, doi:10.1017/S0022278X00016098

Wolpin, Miles D. 1981, Militarism *and social revolution in the Third World.* Allanheld, Osmun Totowa, N.J

Woodcock W, *Short History of Trinidad Volunteers,* Regiment Staff Paper.

Woodis, J. 1978, *Armies and Politics.* Int'l Publishers, New York.

Young, P. & Lawford, J. P. 1970, *History of the British Army,* Putnam, New York,

NOTES